VOLUNTEERS IN LEISURE

A Management Perspective

Ted Tedrick, Ph.D
Temple University

Karla Henderson, Ph.D.
University of North Carolina

Sponsored by the
American Association for Leisure and Recreation
an association of the
American Alliance for Health, Physical Education,
Recreation, and Dance

ABOUT THE ALLIANCE

The American Alliance is an educational organization, structured for the purposes of supporting, encouraging, and providing assistance to member groups and their personnel throughout the nation as they seek to initiate, develop, and conduct programs in health, leisure, and movement-related activities for the enrichment of human life.

Alliance objectives include:

1. Professional growth and development—to support, encourage, and provide guidance in the development and conduct of programs in health, leisure, and movement-related activities which are based on the needs, interests, and inherent capacities of the individual in today's society.

2. Communication—to facilitate public and professional understanding and appreciation of the importance and value of health, leisure, and movement-related activities as they contribute toward human well-being.

3. Research—to encourage and facilitate research which will enrich the depth and scope of health, leisure, and movement-related activities; and to disseminate the findings to the profession and other interested and concerned publics.

4. Standards and guidelines—to further the continuous development and evaluation of standards within the profession for personnel and programs in health, leisure, and movement-related activities.

5. Public affairs—to coordinate and administer a planned program of professional, public, and governmental relations that will improve education in areas of health, leisure, and movement-related activities.

6. To conduct such other activities as shall be approved by the Board of Governors and the Alliance Assembly, provided that the Alliance shall not engage in any activity which would be inconsistent with the status of an educational and charitable organization as defined in Section 501(c)(3) of the Internal Revenue Code of 1954 or any successor provision thereto, and none of the said purposes shall at any time be deemed or construed to be purposes other than the public benefit purposes and objectives consistent with such educational and charitable status.

Bylaws, Article III

CONTENTS

CHAPTER 4

1

VOLUNTEERS AND THE LEISURE SERVICE SYSTEM

O.K., Chief Executive, Assistant Director, or Program Supervisor, so you've managed to survive a few rough years of what might be called "fiscal stringency," or more appropriately "budget havoc," and the docket of things undone remains full. If only there were ways of doing more without hiring additional workers—a rather implausible consideration when maintaining current staffing levels requires daily doses of administrative as well as political savvy. The thought "volunteers" flashes through your mind as a seemingly low/no-cost solution to the dilemma. However, your agency's past efforts to enlist the services of volunteers can best be described as floundering. "Should time allow it," you think, "we really could put our volunteers to better use."

If the comments above are descriptive of how your leisure service organization conceives of, thinks about, or attempts to deal with the volunteers who find their way to your doorstep, then the messages found in the following pages should be helpful. There is a great deal to be gained, both from the agency's and the volunteer's perspectives, by establishing and maintaining a volunteer management system. Like most things in life, the creation of such a system demands planning, effort, and resources, but we firmly believe the rewards will far outstrip the effort expended.

To gain an understanding of the value of volunteers to a leisure service department, the context in which volunteering occurs must be reviewed.

A climate exists which supports, in many ways, the effective utilization of volunteers within leisure service organizations. Sol Cousins, national director of the YMCA, speaking recently on trends and challenges in the industry, identified strengthening the role of volunteer leadership as his organization's number one priority: "Strong, broad-based volunteer leadership ensures that YMCAs are genuinely responsive to community needs" (Ballman, 1988, p. 53). Clearly, it is inaccurate to categorize all efforts, as described earlier, as floundering. There are leisure service departments which have been successful in recruiting, training, motivating, and recognizing their volunteers on a continuing basis.

Among the factors which signal a need to advance volunteerism in parks and recreation entities are resource shortages calling for creative methods of accomplishing tasks, and the attention given the topic on the national level. The decade of the 1980s saw President Reagan create a task force whose purpose was to look at potential avenues for synergism between the private and public sectors. Volunteers, including those who come from private corporations, were viewed as essential in dealing with problems at the local level. The Republican National Committee (1984) published a *Community Partnership Manual* which offered suggestions for creating community task forces to explore issues and establish frameworks for action. After task forces were established, nonprofit organizations would come into play and use their talents to stimulate action. The third component of the strategy was the assistance to be provided through foundations, corporations, and professional associations. The thrust of the program was in keeping with the Reagan Administration's philosophy of constricting the federal role, and the implications for expanded volunteer use were evident.

Likewise, the President's Commission on Americans Outdoors (1986b) strongly recommended that a "prairie fire of action" was needed to deal with the outdoor/environmental concerns of the nation: "Americans working together in their own communities will spark a renaissance for caring about our great outdoors" (p. 49). Volunteerism was an often mentioned theme within the recommendations, and specific guidelines were offered to local communities so that planning could proceed to meaningful action. The concept of a vital "outdoor corps" was stressed, the backbone of which would be volunteers (pp. 69–70). The working documents of the Presidential Commission included one section highlighting 24 successful projects within the country utilizing a variety of community sources and tapping the potential of volunteers (President's Commission on Americans Outdoors, 1986a). It was clear from these recommendations that the United States could benefit greatly if volunteers could be systematically organized and managed at the local level.

We must further realize that volunteers, like the agencies and communities they serve, do gain from their nonpaid efforts.

Some volunteers take satisfaction in seeing improvements in their favorite organization or agency. Others like the personal contact and the opportunity to help others. Many enjoy the spirit of camaraderie that develops when fellow volunteers pull together to achieve an objective. If, then, both individuals and leisure service agencies benefit from a systematic and well-managed volunteer program, a logical starting point for our discussion might be to review the reasons for or the "why" of volunteerism from the organizational perspective.

WHY VOLUNTEERS?

Persons assuming top-level administrative or management responsibilities would be wise to analyze why efforts should be devoted to creating, expanding, or improving their organization's volunteer management system. The reasons most often given for volunteer utilization reveal a rather "selfish" orientation heavily slanted toward the organization rather than toward the individual volunteer: "We use them because we don't have enough full-time staff." "We've always used volunteers; they've coached our youth athletic teams from the beginning." "The courts demand that juvenile offenders participate in community service, so we use them to clean our parks." Such orientations frame the issue from the viewpoint of the department or agency to the neglect of the person who is willing to donate time and effort for personal and institutional betterment. This outlook results in what Ellis (1986) terms "second choice" rather than "first choice" reasons for seeking a quality volunteer management program. As an antidote to a problem, or as something that's been around for a long time, volunteers can be perceived as useful in the short term or simply "tolerated" to some degree by administrators of recreation and parks departments. By negating this tendency to see volunteers only as a potential response to a problem and by foregoing thoughts which center on using volunteers to "make the agency look good," we can start with a clean slate and explore the fundamental question, "why volunteers?"

THE VALUE OF VOLUNTEERS

Assume that your agency's health—budgetary, programmatic and political—is robust. Forget all problems for a moment, and even suspend thoughts of how x action could result in y benefit which would ultimately further your agency's good name. Let us examine some of the "first choice" reasons for considering volunteers.

First, volunteers offer credibility because they are unsalaried. Volunteers engage in their favorite activity without the thought of personal financial gain. The desire is to help others, sometimes specific others such as their children or friends, but the goal is assistance. As such, volunteers are most often viewed by those receiving their assistance as legitimate and sincere. Money does not drive them to do anything in their role, and this freedom often permits a functioning devoid of vested interests or behavior motivated by "oneupmanship" designed to improve one's place in the organizational hierarchy. Service recipients do appreciate this fundamental spirit of volunteerism, and it does lend a type of credibility which differs from that afforded to paid employees.

Consider also that nonattachment to salary permits volunteers to be objective policy makers and ultimately to have great freedom in analyzing the agency's functioning. Since volunteers have no hidden agendas related to pay (they do perceive benefits from what they do, but their agenda is not tied to dollars earned), they can serve as objective evaluators of what goes on in the organization. Likewise, volunteers can be direct, even blunt, in their evaluations, unlike staff, who may fear reprisal for a bold action that could offend those higher up the organizational hierarchy. This factor could divide administrators into two types, those who favor a "bones locked in the closet" approach, which compresses interchange within the ranks under the threat of an autocratic hand, and those who welcome critical self-examination as a means to make improvements. Once in the system, volunteers can provide a self-examination function resulting in constructive criticism. For the openly honest administrator/programmer/supervisor, this is a plus; for others, volunteers may present another threat to what is probably a self-deluded notion of power through the status quo.

Two other benefits offered by volunteers as noted by Ellis (1986) relate to pressures normally associated with full-time employment. Because volunteers schedule their activities around other obligations and commit themselves only to the number of hours they feel they can handle, they often feel less pressure in performing their tasks. Contrasted with a full-time employee who may be juggling a dozen different duties, programs, or deadlines at once, the volunteer understands the level of intensity required for the task and should be in a position in which his or her abilities are in concert with what needs to be done. This sense of control over pressures associated with the workplace can prove very beneficial to both clients and full-time employees.

Another benefit of reduced pressure is that volunteers may be a bit more likely to experiment and try new approaches. Volunteers can be very productive when given an assignment which calls for creative approaches. Regular paid staff may fear failure in such situations, and hence may revert to "safe," uncreative methods, or be so constrained by other responsibilities that the assignment is shortchanged. However, when thrown into a challenge with few competing demands, a volunteer can often devise a creative solution which would not have come from a staff member.

Additional benefits may be directly attributable to the backgrounds of the volunteers. Volunteers represent varied life experiences, specific types of knowledge, and interests that are often directly manifested in the tasks they choose when donating their talents. An axiom from the field of gerontology that applies to volunteers is that older adults are a heterogeneous population comprised of persons who are unalike in many ways because each has accumulated a myriad of personal experiences over their lifetime. Likewise, the athlete who has spent many years in the realm of sports and wishes to share enthusiasm for it, or the devoted reader whose joy is seeing others gain a proficiency with the written word, or the highly visible community organizer whose forte is applying pressure in the right places so that large-scale projects can be attained, each possess special qualities that can turn personal interest into a shared feeling of enjoyment and accomplishment with others. The challenge presented to the leisure service manager is to harness the talents existent in the community served and use them through a well-managed volunteer system.

Volunteers serve another most useful function that should not be forgotten. Because volunteers represent the community from which they are drawn, they can serve as excellent public relations spokespersons for the agency or organization with which they are affiliated (Ellis, 1986). Volunteers who have positive experiences with those they serve are far better ambassadors of the agency than any staff person. Proud volunteers will hail the good works of a leisure service agency—they go out into the community spreading a message which results in an improved image of the organization. Of course, this scenario assumes a positive experience on the part of the volunteer. Administrators who use volunteers must ensure that a system is in place to guarantee their proper selection, training, and placement so that success will be achieved.

An additional benefit of volunteers (Gallup, 1981, 1985) arises from their charitable nature. Volunteers are more likely to support worthwhile organizations financially than are nonvolunteers. In 1985, Gallup found that 92 percent of volunteers also gave financial assistance to charities, and 50 percent gave directly to the agency of their volunteer affiliation.

Administrators need to be keenly aware of these two important areas of support provided by the volunteer—public relations and financial assistance. These are to be valued, especially given the current climate facing leisure service providers.

By way of summary, let us retrace some significant points about the way administrators and other staff view volunteers and their potential benefits to agencies. It was indicated that there can be "first choice" reasons for developing an effective volunteer management program. Frequently, however, it is "second choice" reasons that are at the foundation of the volunteer program, and these "second choice" reasons create a real impediment to the creation of a successful volunteer system. Poor reasons for implementing or continuing volunteer efforts might include: taking them for granted because they've been around for a long time; viewing them as a free labor source, with little regard for the time and resources required to effectively manage them;

or, taken to the extreme, condescendingly accepting them simply because the agency feels an obligation to provide something to do for those who express a desire to volunteer. The overriding philosophy or the "why" of a volunteer management program is often clearly seen in the operational aspects of the system. Its importance cannot be underestimated.

Reviewed were some of the "first choice" reasons for enlisting volunteer support. If these reasons are at the foundation of the system, then efforts are likely to be rewarded by way of people who feel they are achieving both personal and organizational goals. Volunteers possess a certain type of credibility because they are not paid. Their interests and motives are quite apparent and consumers and staff ascribe a legitimacy to their efforts. Volunteers bring special talents, often beyond those of the regular staff of the leisure agency. Clearly, volunteers should never be looked upon to replace staff. There are clear advantages to using paid personnel instead of volunteers. The intent should always be to capitalize on the strengths of those who donate their time so that they complement the roles and duties performed by paid professionals.

Volunteers can and will be objective in a manner perhaps different from staff. They should be able to focus on a specific task and complete it well because the pressure of having to do many things in a short time period does not face them as it does permanent staff. Volunteers are also likely to donate not just time but money, and managers should never forget a volunteer's public relations value. Volunteers can serve as excellent emissaries for the agency when positive experiences are gained through their efforts.

VOLUNTEERING AS A LEISURE PURSUIT

Beyond the issues of benefits to individuals or departments and the reasons for instituting or upgrading a volunteer management system stands a conceptual, even a definitional message which we feel is critical in supporting a leisure service orientation toward volunteer enhancement. The message in its simplest form is that volunteering is a legitimate, desired form of leisure participation by those who select it and, as such, the volunteer participant should receive just as much attention from the departmental staff as any other program or service participant. The goal must be to ensure a quality experience for the volunteer, just as we strive to provide the best environment and leadership for any recreation consumer. In the end, a well-managed, successful volunteer program becomes another opportunity under the umbrella of total leisure activities available.

Readers who have taken any foundation course in a recreation or leisure studies curriculum at the university level will remember the time devoted to defining key terms, such as "recreation" and "leisure." Conceptualizations of time, activity, or experience are discussed in an attempt to have the student seek personal meanings for the terms. The how and why of selecting an experience within a given time block is analyzed, as is the meaning attached to what occurs during that experience. Linking the act of volunteering with these definitional issues of leisure serves to justify concern for volunteer development.

"Time" presents a departure point. It is generally agreed that leisure or recreation takes place only when work and personal maintenance obligations have been met, and thus personal discretion permits one to select an activity for the time block available. Pie diagrams are often visually effective in showing work obligations, personal maintenance such as eating and sleeping, and the remaining "discretionary" period. Under the time paradigm, a volunteer obviously selects a period for involvement which remains after work and personal maintenance commitments have been met. Like recreation, volunteering occurs within one's discretionary time blocks.

Experience analysis is also a fundamental exercise in coming to grips with leisure or recreation. Frequently a number of criteria or qualifiers are associated with notions of leisure or recreation. It must take place during free time, as mentioned above. It must be intrinsically motivated. It must lead to enjoyment or satisfaction. Some claim it must be nondetrimental or positive in a societal sense (however that might be defined). And it must be *voluntary!* Since by definition the act of volunteering meets (or more accurately, seems to revel in) these basic qualifiers of leisure/recreation activity, then it follows that volunteering can be legitimately viewed as a form of leisure or recreation.

The leisure scholars provide further support when definitions are scrutinized. As one example, Godbey (1985) includes within his definition of leisure the following: ". . . to be able to act from internally compelling love in ways which are personally pleasing, intuitively worthwhile, and provide a basis for faith" (p. 9). Isn't a great deal of volunteering motivated by love and directly pleasing to the volunteer? As to being worthwhile, it would seem the scope of volunteer efforts ranges from individual growth to community benefit on a grand scale. Kaplan's (1975) often-quoted definition of leisure offers direct comparisons with volunteering:

> Leisure consists of relatively self-determined activity experiences that fall into one's economically free-time roles and is seen as leisure by the participant, is psychologically pleasant in anticipation and recollection, potentially covers the whole range of commitment and intensity, that contains characteristic norms and constraints, and that provides opportunities for recreation, personal growth and service to others. (p. 26)

Of note, obviously, is the notion of "service to others"; in fact, Kaplan uses the term "voluntariness" to describe the self-determined nature of leisure. The descriptors within the definition appear to be mirroring the basis and outcomes of volunteering.

Research conducted by one of the authors (Henderson, 1979, 1984) further substantiated the conceptual linkage between volunteer engagement and leisure. A study of 200 4-H volunteers revealed a high level of agreement as to leisure components which could also be found in volunteer pursuits, such as the opportunity to provide interaction, the interesting nature of the activity, and the aspect of intrinsic motivation. In fact, 11 out of 13 descriptors were found to be shared when leisure and volunteering were considered. It was noted that volunteers who were highly motivated also tended to perceive their volunteerism as a leisure experience. Marando (1986) also investigated volunteer use in leisure services, and stated that volunteering is a form of recreation to those who choose it. Thus, support is found for the idea that volunteering is a legitimate way to meet leisure needs.

We might also recall Jim Murphy's (1975) concept of leisure as a social instrument. This is a therapeutic approach whereby service agencies, among them leisure organizations, assist those who displayed special needs. The ill and disabled could be recipients under the social instrument view of leisure. Supportive of that concept would be any volunteer who chose to plan, lead, or conduct recreation programs for such clients. Another popular concept advanced by Murphy was the "holistic" approach to leisure where the fusion of work and nonwork was projected because of societal factors. No longer would tightly prescribed parameters define work or leisure. The focus was to shift toward what individuals did and how they felt about those endeavors; it was a concept focused upon "meaningful activity."

While we probably have not achieved this holistic perspective, volunteering stands as an excellent bridge between the work and nonwork spheres. Often volunteers seek the same personal benefits (other than money) found in the workplace, i.e., socialization, working to solve a problem, status within a group, and feelings of achievement; yet the matters of intrinsic motivation, personal enjoyment, and scheduling at one's discretion are associated with leisure. Should changing conditions within society dictate a movement toward a holistic perspective, volunteerism may be one element furthering the transition.

Perhaps even on a higher plane stands the conceptual notion of leisure as a state of being, a condition, a psychological response, or an ideal, all of which can also be linked to volunteering. DeGrazia (1962) comes quickly to mind as an initial proponent of leisure as an ideal that is sought by many but achieved by few. The leisure condition was characterized by feelings of tranquility and peace with oneself. Maslow (1943) included among his higher order needs those of self-esteem, belonging, and self-actualization, all of which have often been mentioned as elements of volunteer motivation. It is conceivable that some volunteers even view their efforts as one method to approach a state of self-actualization. More recently, Gray (1972) challenged us all to conceive of recreation as an emotional condition. Characteristic of this condition were feelings of well-being, mastery, achievement, success, achievement of personal goals, and positive feedback from others. Similar benefits are often mentioned by volunteers, i.e., feeling needed, helping others, helping a friend, interest in an activity (Gallup, 1981, 1985).

So we can see that there is a relationship between leisure as an ideal or condition and how one might seek that state of being through volunteer activity. If the positive condition is built upon a series of satisfying endeavors or accomplishments, these meaningful voluntary pursuits, for some, can be the vehicle to reach the desired state.

THE DEMOGRAPHICS OF VOLUNTEERING

Two points need to be kept in mind as one reviews the who, how much, and where of volunteering. The first is that volunteering, like leisure, exists in a complex sociological, political, and economic environment which at any given time presents problems and opportunities when the demographics of volunteering are scrutinized. Societal phenomena such as increased numbers of females occupying full-time positions, more dual-income families, more families headed by single parents, and the overdone characterization of youth and young adults as being driven only by monetary reward might seem to portend a serious shortage of volunteers. Free time appears to be a very scarce commodity in our society. A Harris Poll (see Hollie, 1985) noted a decline in personal leisure time from 24.3 hours per week in 1975 to 18.1 hours in 1984. However, reported levels of volunteering do not bear out these seemingly apparent negative forces. It appears that many factors are weighed in the decision to volunteer, not the least of which is a commitment to better the human condition in spite of pressing time demands.

The second point to be remembered is that there is no universal definition of volunteering which has been utilized either by those who conduct national surveys or by those who respond to such surveys. Thus, differences in statistics cited can be attributed in some measure to the definition of volunteering that is being employed. In the United States, for example, estimates of how many persons volunteer range from roughly one-third of the population (36 percent in the Gallup Poll, 1986) to just about one-half (46 percent according to United Media Enterprises, 1983). The discrepancy may lie in the form of the question asked, from "are you involved in any charitable or social service activities?" to a broader "do you volunteer?" National surveys have probably underestimated situations where the volunteering has been relatively informal (as in helping clean up a park on a single occasion) or sporadic.

At any rate, it appears that between one-third to one-half of us do donate our talents on a regular basis to an organization in need. Gallup (1986) has noted a steady increase over the years in adult involvement in charitable activity (formal definition used here) from 27 percent in 1977, to 29 percent in 1982, to 31 percent in 1984, to 36 percent in 1986. Another survey undertaken by the Gallup Organization in 1985 which looked at not only charitable organizations but all forms of volunteering placed the figure at 48 percent of persons aged 14 and over. The United Media study (1983) was in near agreement, with 46 percent of their sample, including teenagers, indicating that they volunteered on a regular basis. Gallup (1985) also noted that the average amount of time volunteered was 3.5 hours per week, up from 2.6 hours in 1980.

How might recreation rank as a category of volunteer activity? Gallup (1985) placed recreation fourth as a category with about 10 percent of the total population donating time to recreation agencies (21 percent of those who volunteer give their time to recreation agencies). Recreation trailed religious organizations, education, and fund raising as a category of involvement, and the dollar value of time donated for recreation purposes was estimated at nearly seven billion dollars. If arts and cultural activities were added to recreation, the total worth of volunteer time would be over 10 billion dollars.

The "who" of volunteering offers interesting contrasts when societal trends are compared. As outlined earlier, with the majority of females now in the workforce and the increase in single-parent families, the logical conclusion would be that fewer people, particularly females, would have the time to devote to volunteer activities. However, women continue to volunteer at a higher rate than do males: 51 percent as opposed to 45 percent (Gallup, 1985). When comparing the 1985 survey with one conducted in 1980, Gallup did note a slight decline (5 percent) in female volunteering. However, more significant was the drop in volunteering among persons 18–24 years old (down 11 percent), full-time workers (down 6 percent), and single persons (down nearly 20 percent). In spite of hectic work and family schedules, it is clear that many females value their nonmonetary pursuits and make a conscious decision to volunteer.

The United Media study (1983) found that dual-career parents (59 percent) had the highest level of volunteering among the eight age and family groups surveyed. Volunteerism in a life cycle perspective was characterized as follows:

> Volunteerism is high in the mid-teenage years. It tapers off between the ages of 18 and 34, the years when most Americans are finishing school, beginning careers, and starting families. Volunteerism is highest from ages 35–64, when most Americans have established careers and families, and have settled into their communities as well. After the age of 65 volunteerism tapers off again. (p. 48)

Other socio-demographic variables impacting upon volunteerism are education, income, church membership, and city size: those with higher levels of education and income are more likely to volunteer; church membership is positively correlated with volunteerism; and those living in rural and suburban environments are more likely to volunteer than are those who reside in cities (Gallup, 1981, 1985, 1986; United Media Enterprises, 1983). Although Morgan (1986) has noted that young professionals who work in the city do volunteer in very specific ways, they are most interested in using their specific skills in a productive way and they want to see results. For example, one volunteer used marketing and record keeping skills to reorganize the acquisition and subscription lists of an arts council.

Another fundamental question which has been the focus of researchers and pollsters is, "Why does one choose to volunteer?" The intuitive answer is that there are many reasons why someone might elect to donate her or his talents—a desire to help others or a wish to feel that one is providing a needed service would probably head the list. The benefits received from volunteering may differ, depending upon one's life circumstances and the type of service rendered.

Gallup's (1985) national survey revealed the following reasons given for volunteering: like doing something useful (52 percent), interested in the activity (36 percent), like volunteer work and feel needed (32 percent), it helps a friend or family member

(26 percent), religious reasons (27 percent). Very few respondents listed reasons where personal gain was the primary objective, such as gaining job experience, keeping taxes low through deductions, or simply to fill up free time. Henderson's (1979, 1984) study of 4-H volunteers found similar benefits ("activity was interesting," "provides interaction, cooperation"; "activity is its own reward," etc.). Patton's (1986–87) survey of business people found similar reasons: 62 percent indicated they enjoyed the activity, 55 percent liked helping others, and some felt their volunteering has helped to enhance their company's image. A survey taken of Chicago youth (Popowski, 1985) found that they listed caring about others, caring about their community, and desire to improve their self-esteem as reasons for volunteering. While motivations for volunteering may differ according to the group surveyed, it does appear that helping others and enjoying the activity chosen are prime motivators.

Increasing attention has been given to older adults as a potential and growing pool of volunteers but which so far has probably been underutilized. The theoretical perspective frequently offered is that volunteering could provide a new and particularly meaningful role to the adult who has suffered losses, perhaps through the death of friends or abandonment of the full-time work role. However, an empirical test of the substitution theory conducted by Chambre (1984) found that volunteerism in the elderly was better explained by socioeconomic status, gender, and educational level. In fact, it was suggested that older volunteers may be more likely to have volunteered earlier in life, rather than simply selecting it as an alternative activity in late life. The implication here is that it is best to attract volunteers early in life and maintain their involvement in a variety of tasks throughout their life cycle.

There is a message here for those in leisure service agencies who may come in contact with volunteers: Make the effort to speak to your volunteers and discover why they chose to donate their time. Perhaps the initial interview is the best opportunity. It is clear that the reason that each individual gives should mesh with the duty to which they are to be assigned. As time progresses, check to see if the desired benefits are being realized and if not, take the necessary steps to see that they are.

SUMMARY

A few major themes have been presented in hopes that the reader might consider some of the fundamental issues surrounding volunteers and their management from a system perspective. For many reasons, it would behoove leisure service organizations to develop, maintain, or expand their volunteer programs. Volunteerism has received attention at the national level. Not only does it offer meaning to those who participate, but it enables agencies and organizations to supplement the efforts of their paid workers through the careful selection of tasks suited to volunteer talents.

Leisure service organizations must consider why time and effort should be devoted to the management of volunteers. Volunteers are more than an inexpensive labor pool—they bring special skills, they can be very effective advocates for the agency and its causes, they have inherent public relations value, and they are likely to provide additional assistance to the agency through financial contributions.

Volunteerism was discussed as a legitimate leisure pursuit. Persons opt to volunteer in their free time and they indicate personal gains realized through these endeavors. Persons administering leisure programs should maintain a system which allows volunteers to reach the goals they establish just as they should be concerned with the outcomes of any recreation program.

While it is evident that many people today are overextended in terms of time demands, the act of volunteering is still viewed as significant for the one-third to one-half (depending on the definition or source) of adults who do so. Females, although now working in record numbers, have not abandoned the volunteer role, and currently outnumber male volunteers. Volunteers have expressed personal benefits from their charitable service—helping others, feeling useful or needed, and enjoying the activity chosen top the list.

2

A SURVEY
OF VOLUNTEER SYSTEM
CHARACTERISTICS

A survey to obtain a status reporting of selected volunteer management system characteristics was conducted as a part of this project. The survey was conducted under the auspices of the American Association for Leisure and Recreation (AALR) and its members served as the sample for the study. The AALR members who responded to the survey represent many diverse leisure service organizations: some are employed by local or state governments; some work for profit-making organizations; some are employed by quasi-public organizations funded through a variety of sources; and others serve private, nonprofit corporations or hospitals.

In February 1988, 377 members of AALR were mailed a four-page questionnaire entitled "The Use of Volunteers Within Leisure Service Agencies" (see Appendix A for a copy of the instrument). Four sections were included in the questionnaire. Section I sought information relative to background characteristics of the agency in which the AALR member was employed. Section II consisted of 16 questions that called for yes or no answers on aspects of the volunteer program such as planning time, whether one person served as the coordinator, whether records were kept, etc. In Section III, respondents evaluated different characteristics of their agency's volunteer programs using a Likert scale (strongly agree, agree, disagree, strongly disagree, not sure). Section IV called for open responses to questions about successful roles volunteers were currently filling, areas that could be better served through volunteer use, and new roles that volunteers could assume in the future.

An alpha coefficient of .86 was obtained when the group of returned questionnaires was subjected to a reliability analysis using the Statistical Package for the Social Sciences (Nie et al., 1975). Thus, the questionnaire demonstrated acceptable reliability.

Of the 377 questionnaires which were mailed, 82 were returned. Two were only partially completed and hence were deemed unusable, so 80 questionnaires were used in compiling the data. Budgetary considerations precluded follow-up postcards or other reminders. Although the response rate did not approach 50 percent (a 21.2 percent return rate was realized), the data are considered to be useful, given the exploratory nature of the survey. The reader is cautioned to be conservative regarding generalizing of results to all leisure services organizations managing volunteers. Return addresses showed that responses came from all parts of the country. It was not possible to determine if nonrespondents differed significantly from those who did return a questionnaire.

Among the AALR members who responded, a relatively small full-time staff was the norm. While 42.5 percent said their agency or department consisted of fewer than 5 workers, and 22.5 percent indicated the size to be between 6 and 10, only 15 percent worked for a department or agency with more than 50 full-time staff members.

Variation was seen in the size of the population served as well. Percentages were equally divided between small (fewer than 20,000) and large (more than 251,000) service populations, with 16.2 percent responding to each. Since this question applied only to those who worked for a local government agency, 47.5 percent indicated that the question was not applicable.

The types of agencies represented in the survey were as follows: private, for-profit (8.8 percent); publicly supported, local government (33.7 percent); publicly supported, state government (12.5 percent); quasi-public agencies with mixed funding sources (21.2 percent), and other types of organizations (23.8 percent). Twenty percent also stated that therapeutic recreation was the primary thrust of their organization.

Figure A portrays in bar graph form the responses obtained from questions which focused on selected characteristics of the volunteer management system. The percentage given indicates those agencies in which the given characteristic was present (a yes response). They are arranged in descending order, and it is noteworthy that the graph reveals only one characteristic which exceeded a 50 percent positive response level: that experienced volunteers were assuming more responsibility in the organization (80 percent).

Five characteristics received positive responses in the range of 50 to the low-40 percent levels. These characteristics were: having a written job description for volunteers, providing inser-

Figure A

Characteristics of the Volunteer Program
(characteristic present indicated by "yes" response)

Percent responding "yes"	Characteristic
80.0	Experienced volunteers assume more responsibility
50.0	Written job descriptions for volunteers
48.7	Inservice training provided on a regular basis
43.8	One person assigned as volunteer coordinator
43.8	Formal records kept on volunteers
42.5	Annual records kept on amount of hours volunteered and dollar amount represented
38.7	Adequate time for planning the volunteer program
36.2	Paid staff recognized in assisting volunteer program
30.0	Volunteers given a procedure manual
28.8	Volunteers sign a written contract
28.8	Clear policies on recruiting, assigning, evaluating volunteers
27.5	Volunteers regularly evaluated and meetings held to review progress

vice training, having one person assigned as a volunteer coordinator, keeping formal records on volunteers, and keeping annual records of time volunteered and its dollar equivalent.

At the lower end, or negative side of the scale (all below a one-third positive response rate), were the following: having a procedure manual for volunteers; signing a written contract; having clear policies on recruiting, assigning, and evaluating volunteers; and conducting regular evaluations of volunteers and meeting with them. It is apparent from these findings that, in general, leisure service organizations could benefit through expanded planning and managing activities relative to the use of volunteers.

The characteristics highlighted in this section of the questionnaire are frequently mentioned in the literature as being important in establishing and maintaining a well-run system. While it is probably not reasonable to expect that agencies would respond positively at a level of 90 percent or even 75 percent for most characteristics, with one exception the figures here are at or below the 50 percent level. Only 38.7 percent said that adequate time is spent on planning for the volunteer program. Without more time being devoted to planning and managing volunteers, it is unlikely that most departments will achieve great success with their volunteer program even if its members were to somehow increase by significant amounts. To the contrary, simply having more persons available to volunteer could be problematic if there is no clear direction as to what and how they are to perform and no guidance offered by way of training and meaningful evaluation.

Section III of the survey tool permitted respondents to evaluate on a Likert scale additional components of their volunteer programs. Figure B portrays the positive evaluation ("agree" and "strongly agree" responses were combined) of these components. Appendix B provides the complete breakdown of responses in all categories.

Perhaps of most interest is that survey participants' views of the efforts of their agencies in terms of volunteers fall in the middle of the positive/negative continuum. Nearly half (48.7 percent) agreed they had an effective volunteer program, while a like percentage (47.4 percent) assessed their program in a negative fashion. This finding might serve as a summary of the entire sur-

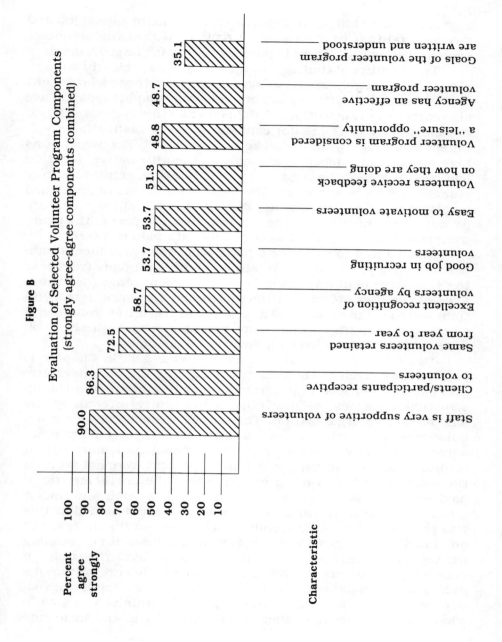

Figure B

Evaluation of Selected Volunteer Program Components
(strongly agree-agree components combined)

Percent agree strongly

Value	Characteristic
90.0	Staff is very supportive of volunteers
86.3	Clients/participants receptive to volunteers
72.5	Same volunteers retained from year to year
58.7	Excellent recognition of volunteers by agency
53.7	Good job in recruiting volunteers
53.7	Easy to motivate volunteers
51.3	Volunteers receive feedback on how they are doing
48.8	Volunteer program is considered a "leisure" opportunity
48.7	Agency has an effective volunteer program
35.1	Goals of the volunteer program are written and understood

Characteristic

23

vey: it appears that some departments are doing a good job and paying attention to a number of aspects within the volunteer system, yet overall, there is plenty of room for improvement.

Two additional findings stand out. Staff are clearly supportive of volunteers (90 percent agreement), and those who benefit from volunteer efforts, e.g., clients or program participants, are also receptive to such efforts (86.3 percent). This bodes well when evaluating one of the major considerations of instituting a volunteer program: "will they make a difference?". The perceptions here answer that question strongly in the affirmative. Mention has been made of the possibility that full-time employees may resent volunteers and even view them as a threat to continued employment; this fear was not displayed in the survey. It is apparent that volunteers can be incorporated as a part of the team, complementing rather than competing with paid workers.

About three-fourths (72.5 percent) of the respondents indicated that they were able to retain the same volunteers from year to year. Agreement was noted in the 50 percent range for the following: whether volunteers were accorded appropriate recognition; whether the agency did a good job in recruiting volunteers; whether it was easy to motivate volunteers; and whether volunteers received feedback on how they were doing.

Two additional findings of interest emerged. In Chapter 1, support was given to the idea of considering the volunteer program as another leisure program similar to athletic leagues, instructional classes, or any other opportunity offered by the leisure service organization. The survey respondents were not quite clear as to whether this was the case. Nearly 50 percent agreed that the volunteer program was another leisure opportunity, 31.3 percent disagreed, and 20 percent were not sure. At the low end in terms of agreement stood the characteristic of having the goals of the volunteer program written and understood by those in the agency. Only 35.1 percent said that this was the case. This finding, coupled with the fact that only about one-third of the agencies are spending adequate time planning the volunteer program, gives the impression that a "system" of organized volunteers is a misnomer for many leisure service departments. The impression is that volunteers are being utilized, but there is a lack of focus on the part of administrators as to what should be accomplished from their efforts, and little concrete attention given to how the agency can respond to those who willingly donate their time and talents. At the core of any task should be a firm understanding of what is to be accomplished, yet this fundamental aspect appears to be missing in a majority of agencies that accept the services of leisure-oriented volunteers.

A final statistical analysis was conducted to determine if selected background characteristics had any relationship to the evaluation of the various management aspects of the volunteer system. The background characteristics used for analysis were: size of the agency; size of the target population served; type of agency (private, public, quasi-public, etc.); and whether or not the agency was primarily offering therapeutic recreation services. These items represented numbers 1 through 4 on the questionnaire. Chi-square analyses were conducted using the Statistical Package for the Social Sciences (Nie et al., 1975). A .05 significance level was employed; strength of association was measured using phi or Cramer's V. Some variables or response categories were combined to reduce the number of cells where no response or number was present.

The "not sure" responses were deleted from the analysis. The categories of "strongly agree" and "agree" were combined, as were those of "strongly disagree" and "disagree." Thus, the analysis was dichotomous in the fashion of simply agreeing or disagreeing with the statement under observation. Some of the background variables were collapsed as well. Size of the population served was divided into 3 groups: 50,000 or fewer; 51,000 to 250,000; and above 250,000. All tables were checked to see that no fewer than 20 percent of the cells had an expected frequency of less than 1.5. See Appendix C for chi-square analyses where significance was found.

In analyzing staff size, one characteristic revealed significant differences. Agencies with fewer than 5 staff members were less likely to evaluate volunteers regularly; medium-sized agencies (11–24 and 25–50 staff) were more likely to evaluate and meet with volunteers. The strength of the relationship (Cramer's V) was moderate (.43).

Significance was found regarding size of the population served and whether or not a volunteer coordinator was utilized. Those serving the largest target population (above 250,000) were more likely to have assigned a volunteer coordinator (.03 significance, strength of association .41 using Cramer's V).

No significant differences were found when responses were analyzed by type of agency, i.e., private, public, or quasi-public. Two areas were found to be significant when therapeutic and nontherapeutic agencies were compared. Therapeutic agencies were found to be more likely to have a volunteer coordinator on hand (.01 significance, .31 phi). Nontherapeutic agencies were more likely to agree that they were doing a good job recruiting volunteers (.05 significance, .26 phi).

SUMMARY OF FINDINGS

The survey was conducted to determine how AALR members perceived various management aspects of the volunteer programs where they were employed. A relatively low return rate (21 percent) was realized from the 377 members who were mailed questionnaires. However, the purpose of the survey was to obtain a baseline about the perceptions of volunteer programs, and readers may find it useful to compare the management characteristics of their volunteer programs with the evaluations of those who participated in the survey. Caution is urged in generalizing, particularly in regard to the chi-square analyses conducted for independence. The questionnaires analyzed did reveal organizations or agencies where the AALR members were employed which represented variety in terms of size, purpose, and organizational background. Respondents used a Likert scale to rate selected characteristics of their volunteer programs and three open-response questions were directed toward areas of current effectiveness and possible roles for volunteers in the future.

Overall, survey participants rated their volunteer programs about in the middle of the positive/negative continuum. A number of management aspects of volunteer programs could be targeted for improvements. At the core would be greater efforts in planning for and establishing goals of the volunteer system. Without attention in these crucial areas, agencies may face a situation where volunteers will continue to be utilized but the impact of their services will not be maximized. On the positive side, 80 percent indicated that experienced volunteers are able to assume more responsibility where they serve. Also, staff are clearly supportive of volunteers (90 percent agreed) and there was a strong feeling (86.3 percent) that recipients are receptive to efforts from volunteers. Nearly one-half of organizations viewed the volunteer program as a leisure opportunity. A summary of the entire survey might be represented by the finding that an equal number of respondents rated their volunteer program as effective as rated it ineffective. The feelings expressed through the questionnaire indicate there is room for improvement in operating volunteer programs within leisure service organizations.

Background characteristics (size of agency, size of target population, type of agency, and therapeutic or nontherapeutic focus) were used as variables in comparing responses to the management aspects of volunteer programs. Chi-square analyses were conducted and a .05 significance level was used. Based upon staff size, one characteristic revealed differences. Agencies with fewer than 5 full-time staff members were less likely to evaluate volunteers than were those agencies who employed from 11–50 people. Agencies serving the largest target population (greater than 250,000) were more likely to have a volunteer coordinator present. Finally, agencies with a public or nontherapeutic focus were more likely to agree they were doing a good job recruiting volunteers than were therapeutic agencies. Public agencies were also less likely to have a volunteer coordinator than were organizations with a primary thrust of therapeutic recreation. Findings from the open-ended responses are discussed in the final chapter.

3

THE NUTS AND BOLTS OF VOLUNTEER MANAGEMENT

Management of volunteers utilizes many of the same practices as management of paid employees. The biggest difference is that volunteers do not get paid for their work whereas employed staff do. The nonmonetary benefit for the volunteers is the personal satisfaction they derive from their efforts. The focus of volunteer management for the recreation, park, and leisure service agency is based on several broad categories:

1. Planning
2. Marketing
3. Placement and Training
4. Supervision and Motivation
5. Evaluation and Recognition

These categories provide a means for understanding volunteer management in general. They are standard to many forms of personnel management and have been particularly useful in the organization of volunteer services. These five major topics will also be addressed based on the importance assigned to them by a group of park, recreation, and leisure service professionals who responded to the AALR survey about the use of volunteers within leisure service agencies which was discussed in Chapter 2. Special issues related to volunteering, such as working with boards and committees and conducting fund-raising campaigns, are discussed in the last chapter.

PLANNING

A volunteer management plan is like a map—it sets the direction for the organization. Park and recreation professionals often do not have enough time for adequate planning, yet planning is integral to the success of a volunteer program. The volunteers, as well as the staff and the community, ought to understand in general how volunteers and volunteerism fit into the entire agency plan. Agency decision makers such as boards and commission members must also know the policies pertaining to selecting, training, and evaluating volunteers. Everyone involved must understand what goals are to be accomplished and how planning objectives will be used to reach those predetermined ends.

In the AALR survey, slightly less than 50 percent of the responding agencies indicated that they felt they had an effective volunteer program. Only 35 percent of the organizations had program goals that were written and understood by all involved. Four out of the ten of the agencies said they had a person in charge who was assigned the role of coordinating volunteers. However, only 36 percent of the agencies indicated that other staff were recognized for working directly with the volunteers. A heartening 90 percent agreed that the leisure services staff were very supportive of the volunteers, and nearly the same percentage indicated that clients and/or program participants were receptive to volunteer staff.

Planning involves developing strategies for what will be accomplished—how, with whom, in what manner, and according to what time frame. Only four out of ten agencies in the AALR study indicated that adequate time was spent planning volunteer programs, thus indicating the need to examine how this might be better undertaken by leisure service agencies.

The most critical aspect of planning lies in determining what value volunteers bring or contribute to the agency. Most people would agree that the primary functions of volunteers are to (a) extend current services, (b) enhance current services, and/or (c) expand services (Institute for Community Service, 1973). The contributions of volunteers must fit into the overall mission of the park and recreation program as well as relate to specific objectives.

Saving money is generally not a valid goal for volunteer programs, although it is often a misconceived benefit. Instead, the focus ought to be on the value of the services provided. In some cases, the volunteer program may, in fact, involve expenditures of direct funds or require the additional use of staff time and energies. Such aspects as insurance, postage, telephone, training manuals and materials, uniforms, provision of child care, fees and tuition, professional development, awards, travel allowances, and indirect costs such as management and supervision, secretarial help, and other overhead can add up to considerable additional expense. The agency must take all these costs into account. The leisure services agency must make a commitment to support volunteers through the coordination role, which does cost monetarily as well as in time and effort.

Another important role related to planning involves the teamwork between volunteers and the other staff in an agency. In some cases there is a real resistance to volunteers among staff. All staff, ranging from the director to the secretaries, maintenance people, and part-time workers, must agree that volunteers have an appropriate role within the leisure services agency. Magoon (1978) has listed a number of reasons why staff may fear working with volunteers:

1. Concern for the client or participant, in that volunteers may not be as effective as staff members.

2. Concern for their own job status—the fear that volunteers may be better than staff and may take away their jobs. (The fact of the matter is that good volunteer programs more frequently have led to the creation of new jobs for people. Volunteers tend to supplement, not supplant staff.)

3. Concern for loss of control—staff fear they will lose their accountability.

4. Fear that community members who volunteer will examine their operations and find they are not as efficient as they thought. (On the other hand, volunteers may take the message back to their friends and families about what a wonderful job the agency is doing.)

5. Fear of change for its own sake.

6. Fear of voicing their concerns.

Each of these apprehensions must be addressed by the staff, and time should be allocated to work through any problems. One must assume that staff experiences are going to be positive and they generally are. However, staff at all levels need to be involved as early as possible in the planning of the volunteer program. The first assessment ought to be of "where the staff is at." If a committee of staff who will be working with volunteers is used, one should make sure the committee is representative of the staff who will be affected by the volunteer program. The staff need to know the goals and objectives for the program and ideally should be involved in the creation of those goals and objectives.

To motivate the staff, it may be necessary to offer several alternatives: make working with volunteers a priority, reward staff formally as well as informally for working with volunteers, provide professional development opportunities related to volunteer supervision, develop a method to provide regular feedback about how staff are working with volunteers from the perspectives of both administrators and volunteers, and develop regular procedures that all staff understand for recruiting, training, and evaluating volunteers.

The overall perspectives may be different, but the goals for the outcomes of the volunteer program should be the same for both the volunteers and the staff. The roles of each and contributions that each can make to the organization must also be understood. Each group needs to consult and share approaches, openly communicate, and nourish mutual respect.

One practical approach to volunteer management planning suggested by Rippel (1978) involves the following steps:

1. List past achievements of the organization.

2. List hopes for the future.

3. List concerns/issues that need to be addressed.

4. List barriers that are thwarting possible achievements.

5. List practical solutions to problems.

6. Gain consensus from the staff.

7. List steps to achieve solutions and how volunteers might assist.

Ultimately the goal of any volunteer program ought to be to design meaningful tasks or opportunities, recruit good volunteers, interview and place persons carefully, and create a climate that allows volunteers to function effectively and creatively. This may be the focus of the leisure service organization or it may be accomplished in conjunction with other organizations or with other government agencies in a community.

What Can Volunteers Do?

Volunteers are different from paid staff in that they value different aspects of a job assignment. In today's climate for volunteering, many possibilities exist for utilizing volunteers in a leisure services agency.

Two major types of volunteerism can be found: structured and nonstructured. These types might also be classified as regular versus lend-a-hand volunteers, or short-term (single event) versus long-term volunteers. Change in the nature of volunteer programs and volunteerism has been largely due to a change in the orientation of people from service-oriented to self-serving volunteer opportunities (Watts & Edwards, 1983). People are looking for volunteer positions which meet their personal needs as well as make a contribution to society.

Within the "formal" volunteer structure, many possibilities exist for how volunteers can help. Volunteers can do administrative work such as involvement with policy-making groups, or office work related to organizational activities. Some volunteers can do advocacy work or lobby on behalf of certain causes. Some can provide technical assistance in areas such as fund raising or another specific expertise. Some can serve as specialists in a particular area, such as a sports program. Others can serve in an advisory or a policy-making capacity.

The most prevalent type of volunteer is the direct service volunteer, such as those who provide group instruction, demonstrations, and one-to-one coaching; develop exhibits, community projects, and special events; provide facilities or funds; help advertise or promote; recruit other volunteers or clientele; train other volunteers; assist with community surveys . . . the list goes on and on. For example, according to a study done by the Minnesota State Planning Agency (1979), activities that volunteers

in parks and recreation enjoyed most were: interpretive programs, planning and management-related assistance, scientific
research and data collection, demonstrations and displays, fire
control programs, and hunter safety instruction.

New ways of volunteering seem to be emerging. Service-
oriented opportunities will continue to be common, but issue-
oriented volunteers are also becoming more prevalent. For example, advocacy has become legitimized, as evidenced by the
strength found in groups such as the Gray Panthers and alliances
formed by special population groups. Community based self-
interest groups such as hobby clubs and athletic clubs are becoming more common. Occupational/self-interest groups such as
professional or business organizations are also becoming
stronger than ever. Some growth seems to be evident in philan-
thropic/fund-raising volunteer efforts. In fact, the Gallup Poll
(1982) revealed that service volunteers are also likely to lend financial support to organizations. However, it is generally better
to separate efforts needed for fund raising from other aspects of
the direct service volunteer management program. (More information on fund raising with volunteers is included in Chapter 4.)

Scheier (1980) has developed ten dimensions which describe
the range of experiences which volunteers are seeking. These
continuums may be useful in planning for the ways in which volunteers can assist a leisure service organization:

- continuous . . . occasional
- as an individual . . . as a group
- direct . . . indirect
- participating action . . . observation
- organized, formal . . . informal, unstructured
- via work . . . via gift giving
- for others . . . for self
- accept system values . . . address system values
- from inside the system . . . from outside the system
- lose money . . . break even

It is the responsibility of the leisure services agency to uncover how these dimensions might be combined to create useful tasks. It is also necessary to consider the specific desires of the volunteer. For example, an elementary teacher may wish to volunteer only for two weeks during the summer with a group of other volunteers. The volunteer coordinator must then figure out how this individual might be accommodated within the framework of the goals of the organization. Sometimes the person responsible for working with volunteers can help a person do great things. John Gardner (1965) summarized it in this way:

> Leaders can conceive and articulate goals that lift people out of their petty preoccupation, carry them above the conflicts that tear a society apart, and unite them in the pursuit of objectives worthy of their best efforts.

At other times, volunteering for an individual can be seen as simply a way to kill time until something better comes along. The professional must be aware of all these possibilities in planning volunteer programs.

Many types of volunteers exist. Some will be committed to long-term volunteering and are content with a structured program and a specific title. Other people are willing to lend a hand when they are asked. The recreation, park, and leisure service provider will need to utilize both types. Management procedures will vary, depending upon the tasks involved and the people who are involved in the volunteer system. Planning should take all of this into account.

Planning Summary

It may be useful to the persons working with volunteers to think about pitfalls that might cause problems in the organization that works with volunteers. When volunteer programs do not work, it is usually due to one or more of these causes:

- The needs of the organization simply cannot be met by volunteers.

- The commitment to volunteers is not shared by staff.
- Staff are not involved in planning.
- Lack of staff training for teamwork.
- Lack of apparent rewards for staff, resulting in poor support for the volunteer program.
- Failure to think goals through.
- A need for better job descriptions and qualifications so volunteers are not over- or underqualified.
- Training is insufficient or inappropriate.
- Recruitment methods are ill-chosen.
- Staff are not prepared to accept responsibility.
- Lack of recognition of volunteer contributions.

The planners of volunteer programs must be prepared for possible problems that arise from costs, the time required for volunteer coordination, a poor match between person and task, wasted talent, overwhelming projects, high turnover and sagging support, overlap in services, and obtaining and paying for liability coverage. Planning may prevent these problems from becoming major obstacles. Preparation is vital to ensure success.

Staff in the Institute for Community Service (1973) suggested several steps that ought to be followed for successful planning:

1. Finish planning before beginning action.
2. Allow time for the planning process.
3. Don't skip steps in planning and develop contingency plans beforehand "just in case."
4. Make a timetable or schedule of events and indicate at what point volunteers need to be recruited, trained, etc.
5. Don't feel compelled to involve a large number of volunteers to be successful—use as many as necessary to reach the goals of the organization.

6. Expect that the volunteer program will improve with experience.

One last activity which may be useful at the outset is to develop a volunteer manual listing the policies and procedures of the organization. Similar procedure manuals are typically used for new full-time staff, and their value has the same extension to volunteers. In the AALR survey discussed in Chapter 2, only 30 percent of the organizations indicated that they used such a manual. However, the development of a manual, while time consuming initially, may be a great help in training and supervision in the future. The manual might consist of the following parts: introduction, department philosophy, organizational chart, list of general volunteer responsibilities, responsibilities of the organization, other volunteer opportunities, demographic or other data about the community or population being served, safety procedures, volunteer forms such as application, records, evaluation forms, etc., and any other specific information for the organization.

In the initial planning, if one keeps in mind the rights and responsibilities of volunteers (see Appendix D), efforts directed toward success may be greatly enhanced. Once the planning is done, it is time to move on to the actual task analysis, position development, and marketing phase of the program.

MARKETING

Marketing offers many applications to be considered in working with volunteers and establishing volunteer programs within leisure service agencies. The challenge lies in how leisure service professionals utilize volunteers to reach the goals of the organization as well as the goals of the individual volunteers. This relates to the transition of potential volunteers to active volunteers. Recruiting is done only after all planning has been completed. Recruiting is only one step in the entire marketing system. Recruitment and marketing, as aspects of the total volunteer management system, are more than merely conveying the message that volunteers are needed.

Fifty-three percent of the respondents in the AALR survey discussed in Chapter 2 agreed that their organization did a good job recruiting volunteers. Less than 30 percent said that there were clear policies about recruiting, assigning, and evaluating volunteers, but over 50 percent indicated that written job (position) descriptions were used.

Marketing is what leisure service professionals use to get potential volunteers to offer their energy, resources, and time (Vineyard, 1984). Marketing is superior to "digging up" volunteers indiscriminately or waiting for them to call. Experts suggest that the aim of marketing is to make selling superfluous by knowing and understanding the customer so well that the product or service fits the customer so well that it sells itself. Ideally, marketing should result in a customer who is ready to buy.

The marketing mix refers to the four Ps: product, place, pricing, and promotion. As a result of careful planning, the product and the place where services are to be delivered should be fairly well known. The pricing will involve the convincing of volunteers (recruitment) that they will receive benefits from their experience. The promotion will be the identification of possible volunteers and the actual advertising of the "product"—the volunteer experience.

Recruitment

According to the Gallup Poll (1985), 10 percent of the volunteers in this country are involved in some kind of recreation volunteering. This is likely to continue in the future. Recreation is an area perceived quite positively as a source of volunteer enjoyment. In the AALR study, almost 50 percent of the respondents in recreation, park, and leisure service agencies indicated that they saw volunteering as a leisure experience and considered it almost like another program offering. Thus, volunteering in recreation activities appeals to an established market that has the potential for continued growth.

Everyone is a potential volunteer. Sometimes volunteer coordinators think there are not enough volunteers; however, many potential volunteers exist who are just waiting to be recruited. Scheier (1978) suggested that "recruiting volunteers is not like finding water in the desert; it's more like controlling Niagara Falls." People are not volunteering any less than they used to, but the number of organizations competing for volunteers has grown dramatically in recent years. Many people think it is more difficult to recruit these days, largely because the "typical" volunteers (i.e., housewives) are not as prevalent as they were. This is not necessarily true, since more working people (including women) are now volunteering (Gallup, 1982). Moreover, the lack of "traditional" volunteers has simply opened the way for other groups to be considered. These will be discussed later in this chapter.

Few easy answers to marketing volunteer programs exist; there are no "quick fix" solutions. There is no easy alternative to an active, ongoing recruitment plan. Further, recruitment can't be isolated from the rest of basic management (Vineyard, 1984). The success of volunteer recruitment depends on having something worthwhile for volunteers to do, identifying sources of volunteers, and getting the message across by asking for help (Ellis, 1985). Recruitment is a form of public relations and must reflect the philosophy and character of the leisure service agency. According to Selvidge (1978), five basic steps are necessary in marketing volunteer programs:

1. Know the product (the volunteer experience and the organization's goals) and have an image of what is needed.

2. Assess the needs based on the organization's mission and goals and the particular objectives of a program, and develop formal or informal position descriptions.

3. Target the audience who may be potential volunteers.

4. Choose a medium or a variety of media for "getting the word out."

5. Sell.

The product that is to be "sold" should have been specifically addressed in the initial planning discussion. The possible roles and tasks for volunteers must then be defined. Can the role be carried out by a volunteer? Is it feasible to train volunteers to do certain tasks? Is it a position that will be interesting and challenging to a volunteer? Will the agency support a volunteer in that role?

One method that may be useful in analyzing the types of volunteers needed could follow the format shown in Appendix E. This worksheet is useful for determining the tasks to be done, the number of volunteers needed, the frequency of participation, the importance of the position, and the expertise required. This assessment of needs should lead to the development of position (job) descriptions for volunteers.

Position Descriptions

Not all volunteers need formal position descriptions, but all volunteers do need direction about what it is they need to do. Position descriptions should be available for all volunteer endeavors to indicate that planning has occurred within the volunteer program. For some types of tasks, the position description will be extremely helpful in identifying what is expected of the volunteer. The position description is an explicit statement of what is involved in the volunteer's role. Recruitment, screening, training, supervising, future planning, and evaluation are based on position descriptions. The position descriptions should be specific enough to describe the tasks that need to be done—the more responsible volunteer positions may need less detail, but they need no less specified direction. Position descriptions should not be too confusing, but they should be explicit. They should contain concrete, easily understood explanations and must reflect the priorities of the tasks that need to be accomplished. Position descriptions are not rules and regulations, but guidelines. They should be flexible enough to be changed as needed. New position descriptions should be incorporated as they are developed within the leisure service organization.

A position description should consist of several components: title, purpose of the position, supervision to be received, time commitment required (both amount of hours and the length of service), qualifications needed, training to be provided, and duties and tasks. Additionally, information might be included about working conditions, expected length of the assignment, and available ancillary experiences. The skills identified or needed may be specialized, technical, practical, human relations, or management/consultative skills. The description should include specific words that describe duties such as accept, administer, advise, develop, formulate, guide, interpret, implement, prepare, review, recommend, recognize, and so on. Appendix F-1 gives an example of a worksheet for a position description which might be used. Appendix F-2 shows an actual position description as it might appear. Based on the position description, one would then move on to targeting the audiences to be recruited.

Target Markets

As was discussed earlier, there are many ways that individuals can volunteer. Efforts will be most fruitful if targeted toward particular groups. A relationship and a congruency between type of person and the position description should be identified. People need to be recognized as diverse and "triangles treated as triangles and octagons treated as octagons" (Minnesota Office of Volunteer Services, 1984). It is also true today that volunteers are becoming more sophisticated. People are coming to volunteer jobs with specific interests and needs in mind.

The "traditional" volunteer of the past has been women who were young to middle-aged and educated. Everyone, however, is a potential volunteer, and professionals in leisure service agencies will need to target specific groups for specific activities. The image of volunteering as something everyone can do should be kept ever present in the minds of both staff and potential volunteers. As indicated before, the structures for volunteering ranging from formal, once-a-week tasks to informal, single-event activities must be kept in mind. The underutilization of certain groups must be a concern for recreation providers. These underutilized groups might include:

1. Older persons who tend to volunteer in small numbers, but who offer a great potential. Retirees and early retirees may be very anxious to volunteer. Volunteering might also be included as an aspect of pre-retirement counseling.

2. Former participants in programs who generally have some commitment to what a particular program or special event has meant to them.

3. Non-joiners who will have to be specifically asked rather than expected to knock on your door.

4. Men who are becoming more evident in volunteering so that today volunteering has begun to lose its sexist connotation.

5. People of all races and income groups who participate in leisure and recreation. Too often we tend to recruit others just like ourselves. It is essential not to overlook people of other races and income levels as potential volunteers.

6. Persons who lack formal education have not tended to volunteer in the past, but they should not be overlooked.

7. The unemployed, for whom volunteering can be a way to gain new skills as well as to fill extra time.

8. Young people, students, and members of youth groups who can contribute a great deal. Do not discount young volunteers, particularly if they can be matched with caring adults.

9. Persons with disabilities who may have just the right talents for certain volunteer activities.

10. Institutionalized persons and people who are undergoing life changes (e.g., divorce, death of spouse) and who can find volunteering a helpful and healing endeavor.

11. Shift workers, weekenders, and those with odd or open schedules who frequently have time when others are

working. Possibilities may exist for those on flex-time or those doing job sharing. Better outreach and target marketing is needed to reach these "non-traditional" people.

12. Families, as groups, where volunteering can be a great family activity as well as a way to get volunteer power. Mothers and/or fathers can have an opportunity to bring their children along, or day care can be provided for small children while the parent volunteers. One possibility is to provide child care volunteers in order to get other volunteers to assist with certain programs.

13. Self-help groups which can be sources of volunteers for any number of activities. The whole area of group volunteering, no matter what kind of group (civic organization, hobby club, etc.), may be a very valuable source of volunteers. Individuals may be recruited from these groups, or the groups can be asked to take on volunteer assignments as a group. Youth groups are one possibility, as are religious groups and social action groups. Local volunteer groups are in a buyer's market—there are so many possibilities which exist for them.

14. Working people who should not be ignored. According to Ellis (1985), every study and poll of the last 20 years has shown that volunteers are likely to be working for pay in addition to volunteering.

15. Corporate volunteers who appear to be a major wave of the future. The mechanics of how these corporate programs work varies from company to company. The overall goal is to help the community. This includes individuals within corporations who receive release time to volunteer, or it may mean actual donations from corporations for direct expenses. These corporate relationships should be carefully nurtured. Further details about corporate volunteering will be discussed in the last chapter.

Once target groups have been identified, the choices of advertising media and promotion can be developed.

Promotion

The purpose of marketing is to bring together people who want a significant experience as volunteers and the agencies who need the volunteers. The specific recruitment of volunteers takes time. Staff in an agency generally will need to allow at least three months to promote any recruitment plan for a particular program or special event—time to get the information out, to enable sources to pass it on, and to have it read, assimilated, and then acted upon (Institute for Community Service, 1973). Staff in the leisure service organization will need to decide whether to recruit program by program, to do a major recruitment effort once a year or seasonally, or to do both. In general, the fall and winter months are the best months for promoting and recruiting. Only about 2–5 percent of the people respond to a general recruitment appeal, so an agency's promotion will need to reach at least 95 percent more people than it actually needs for the volunteer positions (Institute for Community Service, 1973). It must be kept in mind that actual person-to-person contact will yield more volunteers than the most well-organized, flashy mass-promotional effort.

Recreation, park, and leisure services professionals will need to determine what resources exist in the community to help in reaching the targeted volunteers. While specific groups may be targeted, all community groups should know that they are needed and wanted. Community organizations, bulletin boards, and newsletters can be used for general announcements of the need for volunteers. Additionally, it may be useful to develop a worksheet which would identify how particular community groups might be helpful to you. This would include a listing of the type of organization, the contact person, why the members might be interested in helping, the positions required, meeting times, and other pertinent information. A sample worksheet is given in Appendix G.

As a volunteer coordinator, remember that it is usually better to actually *ask* someone to help than to expect high caliber volunteers simply to show up. People most often volunteer because they are asked. Experience has shown that less than 5 percent of the volunteers walk into an office and offer to help

(Institute for Community Service, 1973). The best recruiting frequently occurs informally by satisfied volunteers—they tell their friends or invite them along to participate. Certain people can become contacts for recruiting persons they know or work with.

The medium that is used for promotion and recruitment must appeal to people's motivations. As mentioned earlier, personal contact is the best way to get volunteers, whether it is done by the recreation staff person or by another volunteer. It might be best to think, "How would I like to be approached about being a volunteer?"

A number of agencies have been successful in using recruitment teams. These teams can work in a number of ways. A committee is generally formed which analyzes the tasks needed, develops materials, sets time lines, assigns territories or jobs, advertises, monitors, and plans. Informants might also be useful. Informants tell where potential volunteers are and might include mail carriers, bartenders, police officers, adult educators, clergy, bus drivers, and other such groups.

A recruitment drive might be used as a broad based publicity tactic. This involves getting other groups involved, and provides a focus for a volunteer marketing campaign. The drive might be organized by a committee of volunteers or by agency staff. Trigger events can be developed to highlight the need for volunteers. These events occur in the hopes that if a person hears about something enough and is triggered to think about it, he or she will eventually volunteer (Chambre, 1982). An example would be to focus major efforts on a group intensely for a week, including all forms of media—flyers, posters, meetings, public service announcements—so that individuals will hear about an opportunity several times.

A good volunteer recruitment brochure can be very helpful. A sample layout for one is included in Appendix H. The brochure should include a description of what the position or positions involve(s), training and supervision needed, necessary requirements and qualifications, and list of dates and deadlines. The brochure must provide adequate information about the tasks and positions because it is a part of the initial screening process. One brochure could be prepared for a particular position, and another, more broad-based brochure outlining the agency's variety of volunteer opportunities could also be developed.

Posters placed strategically in banks, movie theaters, elevators, laundromats, supermarkets, waiting rooms, the corner bar, drug stores, elevators, libraries, gas stations, and restaurants can be effectively utilized to recruit volunteers. Billboards are another possibility.

Cable TV and other mass media are now used more frequently for recruiting volunteers. The leisure service agency might run ads on a local cable channel or in the local newspaper giving a "wish list" of projects the agency would like to have done, or the kinds of equipment it needs. This wish list might include such projects as cleaning up parks or performing particular office tasks. Public service announcements on radio or television might also be beneficial.

Another way to promote volunteerism is to have a meeting or an open house. Although this can be useful sometimes, it is generally better if the professional makes a direct appeal to people at meetings of specific groups like church groups, civic clubs, and other community organizations. The leisure service staff member can ask for 5–25 minutes to describe the kinds of programs being done, the help that is needed, and how people can get involved. The leisure service staff member can recruit individuals for a project or try to enlist the help of the entire organization.

News releases can be useful in targeting particular groups. However, a more successful approach is to try to get a special interest story about a particular volunteer or a unique program offered by the organization that utilizes volunteers. Human interest stories have far greater appeal to the public, and the newspaper is more likely to print them rather than a general announcement.

Additional places where one can go to recruit volunteers are colleges and universities, labor unions, government agencies, businesses, and community agencies. Sometimes joint projects can be identified that benefit the leisure service agency as well as the community or government agency. For example, promotional efforts can be coordinated with the Welcome Wagon representatives or with Parent Teacher Organizations. Bumper stickers, pencils, and other handouts are a good way to call attention to your organization and its need for volunteers.

The use of videos, slides, direct mail, telethons, and volunteer fairs are also effective ways to find volunteers. Church bulletins are another. If the community has a Voluntary Action Center, the Center can be very useful in publicizing the volunteer needs of the leisure service organization, and may even be willing to help by screening volunteers.

No single medium will work with all targeted groups for all projects. The leisure service provider needs to choose those that fit the budget and that are most likely to get results. Selling is the next critical step.

Selling and Getting People to Sign Up

The final step in the marketing procedure related to volunteers is to sell them on the idea. This involves getting them to "sign on the dotted line." Once the promotional techniques elicit an inquiry, it is important to respond immediately. The steps include preparing, approaching, presenting the material, and closing the deal (Robins, 1982). It is important to be honest and not to oversell. Stress the idea that something good will happen to the person when a mutually agreeable assignment is negotiated. Some practical considerations include:

- Sell personally; do not wait until the last minute to get the volunteer's commitment.

- Make sure the volunteer knows about the organization.

- Tell the volunteer why you are involved.

- Share the position description as formally or as informally as it is written.

- Emphasize how and why the person is needed.

- Show how the volunteer will be assisted with training and supervision.

- Tell what qualifications are being sought.

- Do not minimize the task to be done unless it really is a minimal task.

- Ask the person to apply.

- Explain the procedure for how decisions will be made and what future communication to expect.

Volunteer coordinators are most successful at getting people to say yes by telling them what is expected, breaking a large job into smaller pieces, being specific rather than general, asking for a definite short-term commitment, being complimentary and not apologetic, being friendly and sincere, having a specific purpose in mind, offering a challenge, and making the task achievable. The seller must be persistent yet patient. The ultimate goal is to get the potential volunteer to apply for the position.

The application enables the agency to acquire information about the volunteer's particular experience and skills. A sample volunteer application is given in Appendix I. In some cases a formal interview should be held before placement. In other cases the application is sufficient to ensure that the volunteer's needs and abilities match the agency's needs and goals.

A final note about marketing concerns retention of the volunteer workforce. Retaining volunteers is the most cost-effective way to build a program (Acker, 1983). The use of appropriate training, good communication and supervision, and meaningful recognition are the best ways to keep volunteers. Almost three-fourths of the respondents in the AALR survey indicated that they were able to retain volunteers year after year. Most social service agencies, however, do not do a very good job of trying to maintain volunteers (Watts & Edwards, 1983).

The more volunteers are retained and given additional responsibilities in the agency, the less new marketing that needs to be done. Eighty percent of the staff in the agencies involved in the AALR study stated that they provided opportunities for experienced volunteers to assume greater responsibilities. It must be kept in mind, however, that new volunteers are continually needed, and retention can become detrimental if volunteers are not given new challenges and opportunities to grow. Helping volunteers to move on to new experiences within the agency or outside of the agency will enhance both the contributions they make and their feeling of accomplishment.

Park, recreation, and leisure services staff must continually keep in mind the barriers which prevent people from volunteering. There might be personal barriers such as lack of transportation, physical disabilities, conflicting work schedules, or lack of child care, or institutional barriers such as parking problems, lack of training materials, inconvenient time schedules, or lack of information. Staff in leisure service agencies should address the institutional barriers directly and try to create solutions to the personal barriers. Any barriers which exist should be addressed as a part of the ongoing marketing program. Staff should promote the benefits of volunteering and be "user-oriented" (Vineyard, 1984) in all their marketing activities.

PLACEMENT AND TRAINING

Placement and training is the third major dimension of volunteer management. This includes the aspects of interviewing, placement, and training in the form of job orientation, on-the-job training, and continuing education. Interviewing and placement are phases of marketing as well as initial processes in training volunteers.

About one-third of the agencies responding to the AALR survey indicated that all volunteers sign written contracts, and almost half indicated that they used inservice training on a regular basis in working with volunteers.

If marketing and promotional techniques have been successful, potential volunteers are interested in the organization and a specific volunteer opportunity within it, and have filled out an application. Interviewing is the next step.

Interviewing

A formal interview, especially for a long-term volunteer position, helps ensure a proper match between the volunteer's abilities and the agency's needs. There is a danger in working with volunteers that they will perceive their work as a waste of time, that their skills will not be used properly, or that jobs will not be suited to their talents. It is also possible that, in a volunteer co-ordinator's enthusiasm about "selling" the volunteer position, the entire truth has not been told. The purpose of the interview is a final opportunity for both the volunteer and the agency to decide if the union will work. Ideally, both arrive at the same conclusion after the interview.

Interviewers must have positive attitudes about themselves, the organization, and the value of volunteers. They must be open, sensitive, and honest. Interviewing is a complex and challenging skill. Individual interviews are the ideal, but it is possible to do them as a group. The interviewer must ask appropriate questions and listen actively. The interview should be conducted in a professional manner, with a set appointment and within a specified time frame. No promises should be made that cannot be carried out. The interview is often the first step in orienting the volunteer to the leisure service organization. The interviewee is "checking out" the professional and the agency just as the interviewer is "checking out" the potential volunteer.

The three major goals of an interview are to establish a friendly relationship, to secure information from the prospective volunteer, and to disseminate information about the position and the agency. One of the purposes of the interview is to determine the needs of the volunteer. Often the volunteer does not know exactly what he or she needs or desires. The interview helps to identify specific interests and to discover or clarify the skills and potential of the individual. The interview should bring together the requirements of the position and the qualities and goals of the applicant.

The volunteer's needs can be determined in the interview by covering such topics as:

- What do you want to gain?

- What did you like best about your last volunteer position?

- What did you like least about it?

- How did you hear about this position?

- What kind of people do you most like to work with?

- What gives you the greatest satisfaction in life?
- Why did you choose to come here?
- What do you do for leisure?
- Describe your work habits.
- What makes you angry?
- Tell me about your family.
- Are you more of a task-oriented person who relishes getting a job done, or are you more the people-oriented type?

It is essential in ending an interview that the person knows exactly what will occur next. The interviewee needs to know on what date they will hear if they have been chosen, on what date they will begin, specific dates for orientation or training, and any other information that is critical to the position.

Placing Volunteers

With the use of position descriptions and target marketing, matching volunteers to appropriate tasks is simplified because volunteers can be specific about what they want and need. It is still necessary, however, to ensure proper placement. It is better to have a position just a little bit more challenging than the skills of the volunteer so as to hold the person's interest than it is to have the position be too easy and therefore become boring. Appendix J illustrates pictorially the need for challenge.

When evaluating a volunteer for placement, it is best to consider availability and flexibility, source of interest, attitude toward the clientele, self-concept and personality, growth potential, and the overall subjective evaluation of the interviewer (Institute for Community Service, 1973). If compatible placements are made in the beginning, problems are less likely to occur later on.

The agency's expectations for the volunteer should be made clear; likewise, what the agency will provide must be stated in unambiguous terms. If one position does not work for a volunteer, he or she should be encouraged to try another assignment or another agency. A volunteer agreement form such as the one shown in Appendix K can be a useful tool to use along with the position description. The agreement should stipulate clearly the duties and manner of accomplishing the volunteer assignment and the assistance that will be received from the agency.

Once the interviewing and placement are completed, the volunteer should be notified that he or she is accepted. It is preferable to notify the person in writing so that information can be included about the training program that will follow.

Training and Orientation

Volunteers do not come to most programs "ready made." Training is necessary to enable the volunteer to learn about the role, agency, and clientele in more detail. Training should also offer an opportunity for personal growth and a chance to identify and discuss specific questions. The purpose of training is to extend horizons, encourage competency, build confidence, and share in new discoveries. Training is not only desirable but necessary for most volunteer positions in park, recreation, and leisure service agencies. Not only can skill development, knowledge, and agency or client information be given in training, but it also can lead to better working relationships with the paid staff.

It is difficult to train by mail, although it may be adequate for some simple tasks. One-on-one training is best.

Generally, training consists of three dimensions: (a) orientation, which can be done when a volunteer first begins work or prior to the initial starting date and involves providing an overview and introduction to the agency as well as to the specific job; (b) on-the-job training, where a volunteer learns specifically what he or she is to do and is given supervision so that major problems are avoided; and (c) continuing education, where specific topics, workshops, or meetings are presented for general knowledge, skill development, and personal growth during the person's tenure as a volunteer.

Many techniques exist for training. In some cases, training

can be done in conjunction with other agencies. In parks and recreation, for example, board and commission members are sometimes trained along with those from other cities in regional or state-sponsored meetings. Most of the time, however, training is the responsibility of the leisure services agency staff.

Trainers (agency staff) must believe in the value of volunteers, have an understanding of group processes, and know how the agency and its personnel function. The purpose of the training session should be clearly stated as to whether it is educational, for information dissemination, for decision-making and planning, or geared toward team development. The methods chosen will vary depending upon the purpose of the training. The trainer should consider whether he or she is the best person to do the training, if the training is congruent with the goals of the organization, if the training promotes participation by the volunteers, and how best to accomplish the agency's goals.

A good learning experience will result from openness, mutual trust, mutual respect, mutual concern, challenge, and excitement. Since most volunteers are adults who are voluntary learners, they will reject learning experiences if they are not satisfied by them (Knowles, 1970).

Learning can be divided into at least two types, pedagogical or child-centered, and andragogical or adult-oriented. The implications for training adults based on principles of andragogy include:

- Recognize and use varied life experiences.

- Structure the training around the volunteer's needs.

- Develop learning experiences related to the problems and concerns of the volunteer and make them timely.

- Help the volunteer to be self-directed.

- Plan for the productive involvement of the volunteer.

- Provide a framework for the volunteer to be ready and anxious to learn.

- Foster equality and mutuality.

- Make the trainer and trainee equally responsible for the outcomes.

The trainer should create and maintain a learning environment focusing on the goals at hand, present information as needed, process information and pull from all volunteers' perspectives, direct and monitor the activities, and manage the individual participation (Schindler & Chastain, 1980).

The trainer(s) should be chosen wisely, staff in the agency should be involved, both humor and seriousness should be used, and a relaxed atmosphere should be facilitated. It is often helpful to use handouts, personal experiences, socializing opportunities, group participation, time for practice, modeling behavior, and respect for individual styles (Schwartz, 1982).

In a nutshell, training consists of establishing a learning climate; achieving goal agreement; conducting the learning activities using appropriate formats, methods and techniques; and evaluating the training experiences. The focus of training will depend upon the particular volunteer position descriptions. Cognitive training might be useful, wherein knowledge and understanding are the aim. Affective training involves looking at values, attitudes, and beliefs. Skill training consists of developing or perfecting the specific techniques called for by the position description.

The timing and setting for the training can affect its outcome. Training should be conducted as needed, such as monthly, or semiannually. The setting is very important. If the meeting can be held at the leisure service agency's offices, it often helps make volunteers feel a part of the entire office staff. The use of moveable chairs is most effective for the types of training done with volunteers. The time of day, day of week, time of year, length of session, and frequency of sessions must be carefully considered to ensure they meet the needs of the people who volunteer. The meeting should be as convenient as possible and not too long—no more than 2–3 hours. A list of additional considerations when choosing a training setting is given in Appendix L. Jorgensen (1980) proposes the following 14-step method for training volunteers:

1. List the tasks you want the volunteer to perform.

2. List the specific knowledge the volunteer must have.

3. Develop specific learning objectives.

4. List the content to be taught.

5. List the teaching methods possible.

6. Select the best teaching method.

7. Estimate the time needed to do the training.

8. Decide what to do in orientation.

9. Decide what to do in inservice training.

10. Develop the training program format.

11. Determine the training materials required.

12. Identify the personnel to use.

13. State how you intend to evaluate.

14. Do the training, amend, and try again.

If the training session is long, vary the methods used. The methods selected should maximize the abilities of the trainer and should keep the volunteers involved. Create initial enthusiasm for the training. Use an outline; be seen and heard; talk in simple words and avoid agency jargon; tell, show, repeat, and encourage learning by doing; move with confidence; use humor. Remember that both staff and volunteers are teachers and learners at any given time.

A variety of specific methods can be chosen for the volunteer training. These include lectures, slides, debates, guest speakers, videotapes, audiotapes, packaged programs, demonstrations, readings, brainstorming, field trips, listening teams, experience sharing, buzz groups, problem solving, panel discussions, negotiations, reporting out, guided discussions, role playing, case studies, critical incident processes, socio-dramas, and in-basket exercises. The possibilities are numerous. Don't overlook the fact that other volunteers might serve as trainers and share their various skills with new volunteers.

Orientation and continuing education training which is done properly has a multiplier effect and will spread throughout the group. The greatest reward of training is the opportunity to see people grow and develop.

Training should always be evaluated to see if it was useful

and to determine whether things ought to be done differently next time. Evaluation can be done by giving volunteers a question-naire at the end of their time with the organization or by going through a checklist such as the one in Appendix M.

One final word about training involves other staff in the agency. Staff should be an integral part of the training. Involve-ment will help them feel a part of the process and will also give volunteers a chance to get to know the staff better. The staff also must be well informed and motivated so they can effectively work with volunteers. It has been said that the best way to learn is to teach—while doing training, staff also are being trained. As with any other part of the volunteer program, if training is to be ef-fective, it must be a team effort, and all staff who have contact with volunteers ought to be involved.

SUPERVISION AND MOTIVATION

If volunteers are well trained, supervision will be much easier. The purpose of supervision is not to constrain the volunteer, but to provide guidance, encouragement, support, and sometimes ad-ditional on-the-job training. Supervision is the process through which the volunteer is given guidance which will enable him or her to perform assigned tasks more efficiently and effectively. Supervision should help the volunteer to maintain interest and enthusiasm for the job. The emphasis on supervision should be on developing a strong working relationship with volunteers. The failure of most volunteer programs is usually due to poor super-vision. Walt Disney described supervision best when he defined management as "getting work done by developing people, while having fun" (Kennedy, 1985). The leisure service provider su-pervising volunteers is managing a "talent bank"—what could be more exciting?

Several components are involved in volunteer supervision. These include general supervision, communication, motivation, record keeping, and disengagement. Each of these will be dis-cussed as they apply to volunteer management.

Over half of the recreation, park, and leisure services professionals who responded to the AALR survey discussed in Chapter 2 agreed that the volunteers in their agencies received feedback concerning how they were doing. Slightly more than half indicated that it was easy to motivate volunteers to do their tasks. Less than half of the respondents indicated that they kept formal records on all volunteers and that the agencies kept annual records concerning the amount of hours volunteered and the dollar amount that time represented. These results indicate that attention is being given to volunteers by some leisure service agencies, but there is a need for more efforts in supervising and record keeping.

General Supervision

Effective supervision is expected by volunteers. If a great deal is expected from volunteers, they will usually live up to it. A leisure services professional should not lower standards just because the people involved are volunteers and less is expected from them than from paid staff.

Supervising volunteers takes time. Volunteers are not "free help"—they require expenditure of time and energy for effective supervision. If supervision takes more time than the payoff in results, then perhaps the agency should reconsider volunteer recruitment or align volunteers' tasks with a supervisory style which is reasonable from the agency's perspective. In most cases, however, volunteers are more than worth the time it takes for planning, marketing, training, and supervision.

Today's enlightened supervision or management is just as concerned with the strengths of the volunteer as with any other aspect. The focus in this type of supervision is on positive feedback, reassurance, and reinforcing the volunteer on what is being done properly rather than pointing out weaknesses. A focus on continuous innovation, renewal, and rebirth is necessary in supervising volunteers. A fine line exists between too much supervision and too little. The climate of the organization must be one that fosters trust and caring, and commitment and hard work are necessary for the program to be effective. In addition, the lines of authority must be defined so that accountability is possible.

In general, supervision involves helping people understand what is expected of them, guiding them in doing their work, recognizing good work, providing constructive criticism when necessary, helping them accept greater responsibility, encouraging them to improve themselves, and providing a safe and healthful environment. Supervision should be scheduled regularly, should pertain to the volunteer assignment, and should not differ from other supervision. Supervision should be planned and carried out early in the volunteer's assignment. Management by persuasion rather than coercion is essential (Wilson, 1984). Participatory leadership is the key.

It takes interdisciplinary skills to be an effective volunteer supervisor. In fact, some college curricula are now preparing professional volunteer managers who possess the needed skills. To be an effective supervisor of volunteers, one must be able to deal with and lead people, possess problem-solving skills, be able to delegate responsibility and manage by exception, and be able to manage time. The volunteer supervisor must know what is expected of volunteers, keep adequate records, provide meaningful and challenging tasks which accomplish goals, find ways to quantify nonfinancial contributions, ensure an institutional commitment that makes volunteer assignments work, communicate with volunteers often and honestly, and provide meaningful recognition (Gibson, 1986).

Communication

A major part of supervision is communication. Feedback must be systematically given. Volunteers need to be heard. A participatory style of communication is most effective when it allows give and take in talking. One of the major reasons why people leave volunteer positions is because of poor communication (Proudfoot, 1978). The biggest problem between staff and volunteers is frequently the lack of communication. Communication must take time, must be continuous, and must be sensitive. The volunteer's time must be respected, since volunteers often are very busy. Many times it is useful to treat the volunteer as you would a co-worker.

Communication can occur in the form of individual conferences, group conferences, and telephone contact. The key is that it must be constant and must reflect the needs of the volunteer. Some communication can be handled effectively by mail, written notices, or newsletters. However, a leisure service staff member cannot rely on written communication as the sole means of providing communication.

Motivating the Volunteer

Volunteer motivation ought to be a duty assumed by the volunteer supervisor and all other leisure services staff. Three points occur when volunteer motivation is paramount: (a) at the outset phase, when a potential volunteer decides to volunteer and begins the assignment; (b) during the stability phase, when the volunteer must maintain enthusiasm for the position; and (c) at the drop-off phase, when the volunteer wants to quit or to move on to something else.

Motivation is like the two blades of a scissors—one blade is the individual and the other is the organization, and motivation involves the coming together of the two (Wilson, 1976). Motivation is the process of meshing individual goals with group objectives.

A number of motivational forces are occuring in volunteers. Some of these forces say yes and others say no. There are internal forces, interpersonal and group member forces, and situational forces (Schindler-Rainman & Lippitt, 1971). Most volunteer activity is a result of multiple causation, with altruism as a very minor factor (Gidron, 1983). Many people are interested in the self-actualizing possibilities of volunteering as opposed to "repayment of debt." People are oriented toward their own learning, growth, and excitement. People are conscious of an inner orientation. They come not necessarily with overflowing altruistic motives, but a need for self-growth, work experience, self-esteem, enjoyment, relationships with others, contributing to goals, and affiliation (Briggs, 1982). Supervisors working with volunteers need to spend time finding out which forces are driving the individual volunteer, and then help volunteers to meet those needs within the context of the organization's goals. If the volunteer's agenda matches what is possible within a volunteer position, the experience is likely to be mutually satisfying.

In his 1982 study, Briggs found that most volunteers were satisfied with their jobs (and thus motivated to continue) if they were doing things that made them feel good about themselves, if the staff members were friendly, if they got respect from staff, and if they were recognized for doing their jobs well. The supervisor must minimize the amount of compromise between what volunteers consider most important and the satisfactions they receive. For example, some aspects of a particular volunteer position may not be the most fun, but a supervisor can help emphasize how important those tasks are to the organization and thus help the volunteer find some satisfaction in doing them.

Many persons have developed theories about motivation, primarily in the workplace. These theories can be applied to the supervision of volunteers. Most emphasize the need to try to match volunteer needs with organizational needs and then provide a way to recognize volunteers for their efforts. Volunteers may be additionally motivated by job enrichment and job enlargement, particularly the volunteer who has reached a plateau and is ready to assume a larger, expanded role. To be adequately motivated at all phases, a volunteer needs a job where self-expression is possible (Gidron, 1983).

In summary, to best motivate volunteers and to keep them motivated, Kennedy (1985) suggests that volunteer supervisors provide volunteers with a big picture of what the agency is trying to accomplish and let them see how their tasks fit into that picture, help them to find self-esteem in their work, empathize rather than sympathize, provide legitimate training, provide recognition, and set an example.

Recordkeeping

Recordkeeping is another critical role of the volunteer supervisor. Records can tell about a volunteer's profile, can be a planning tool for training, and can help to determine how to plan the volunteer program in general. Recordkeeping is often one of the weakest aspects of a volunteer organization. What a supervisor chooses to record shows what is worth noting about what the volunteer does (Honer, 1981). Records also provide baseline data to be used in writing proposals, doing evaluations, and documenting services.

The data recorded may relate to whatever the agency considers important: hours worked, training undertaken, supervision notes, recognition given, questions asked by the volunteer, and other such data. To be most effective, the records should be meaningful, appropriate, congruent, timely, and serve some useful purpose. Both formal and informal notes concerning personnel may be kept. Appendix N shows a sample record that can be kept for an individual volunteer.

With the use of data-based systems on computers, it is easier today than ever before to keep data, manipulate it, and use it. Data-based management systems are numerous for micro- and mini-computers. Data-based programs can be set up similar to handwritten records and can provide a means for more quickly analyzing quantitative data such as number of hours volunteered. Whatever the method, handwritten or computerized, some uniform system of recordkeeping should be used throughout the leisure service organization.

For the volunteer, agency records allow access to what he or she has done. The records can be useful for determining tax deductions or for insurance/liability purposes. A record of training received can also be useful to the volunteer if at some later date he or she needs a recommendation.

Supervision and Disengagement

Volunteers will eventually decide to disengage from their organizations, regardless of how good the supervision has been. This is a positive happening because it allows for new people to come in and assist. Volunteers should not stay indefinitely. Park (1984) suggested that perhaps there should be four Rs of volunteering—recruitment, retention, recognition, and release.

The supervisor should conduct a periodic formal review with the volunteer to determine how he or she is doing. The volunteer should feel that it is not impossible to move on to a different volunteer experience or agency. Volunteers should be encouraged to look for job enlargement and enrichment activities.

Sometimes volunteers change their minds because their expectations are not met, they lack appreciative feedback, or the working conditions are not good. Sometimes there is a change in the volunteer's personal situation or the volunteer is not performing as adequately as he or she would like. It is possible that an unrealistic expectation existed from the beginning as to what would be accomplished and how the volunteer would be received. The volunteer supervisor needs to try to find out why a volunteer is leaving so that steps can be taken to correct any problems that could cause the premature exit of other volunteers. Turnover is only bad when it is unanticipated, untimely, occurs frequently, or when time is wasted decrying it (Park, 1984).

Sometimes it is necessary to ask a volunteer to resign or to leave an agency. To prevent this difficult situation from happening, it is important to know the types who are least likely to work out—no shows, procrastinators, know-it-alls. Sometimes instead of firing a volunteer, she or he can be reassigned. At other times the volunteer just does not fit into the organization, and he or she needs to know this.

If it becomes necessary to release a volunteer, several aspects should be taken into consideration. First, establish clear parameters for what the performance ought to be and refer to the position description and written contract if necessary. Second, ask yourself what the consequences are going to be, from both the agency's and the volunteer's perspective, if you fire the person or if you do not. Clearly, leisure service providers should not be in the business of shattering egos, yet if performance has been woefully inadequate or the volunteer has had unrealistic expectations, then it will be a disservice to both the agency and the individual to continue a relationship that is obviously not working out. It is most important to try to help the volunteer correct the problem. Otherwise the individual should be helped to find another position. The volunteer should be corrected in private, and all efforts should be made to try to understand the volunteer's point of view. It is important to be as constructive and specific as possible with the volunteer.

Appendix O offers a brief quiz which may help leisure service staff members identify how well they are doing on various aspects of volunteer management. The AALR survey asked a number of these questions, and they provide some sense of how professionals in recreation, park, and leisure services perceive volunteer management. Although it appears that some leisure service agencies are doing a very good job, room for improvement is evident. The "bottom line" suggests that the volunteer coordinator must be a continuous example of communication and commitment to the work with volunteers.

EVALUATION AND RECOGNITION

Evaluation is the process of determining whether or not a volunteer program has been successful, where problems exist, and what can be done to improve the program. Evaluation means examining the quality of a volunteer program by measuring its effectiveness in both qualitative and quantitative terms. Recognition of volunteers is closely tied to evaluation as leisure service providers try to discern what impact the volunteer program has had and how those who have been responsible can be rewarded. The purpose of both evaluation and recognition in the most idealistic sense is to strive for a perfect organization, a perfect administration, and for perfect volunteers.

Only a quarter of the recreation, park, and leisure service respondents to the AALR survey indicated that they had a system for regularly evaluating volunteers. Almost 60 percent, however, agreed that their volunteer recognition was excellent.

Evaluation

Three aspects of the volunteer system must be considered in evaluation: the volunteers themselves, the actual program and whether or not its objectives are being accomplished, and the supervision of the program. Each needs to be considered in a systematic manner.

To be useful, evaluation must be practical, efficient, and appropriate to the particular setting. Evaluation should be done in a spirit of honesty and sincerity, should demonstrate which goals have been reached and which have not, and must be used simultaneously with planning. Evaluation can help to organize and focus the commitment toward volunteers by demonstrating or quantifying worth. The evaluation can act as a catalyst for other activities, and can be used to challenge and achieve consensus. For example, by struggling with a problem concerning why something did or did not work, new solutions can arise that volunteers and staff agree are better than previous modes of operation.

Evaluation may be done by the supervisor, the staff, the volunteers, the community, or a combination of all of these groups. Three basic steps are involved in any type of evaluation system: determining criteria, collecting data, and making judgments and interpretations of the data. No generally accepted guidelines exist for how to evaluate specific volunteers or how to evaluate volunteer programs in general. Some general questions to consider are: Is the volunteer learning from the assignment? Does the agency show progress toward its goals? Has the community gained? Has the organization gained?

One approach to the evaluation process includes identifying program objectives, deciding how to determine or measure whether the objectives were met, designing and implementing an instrument, determining who will answer the questions and when they will be answered, and ascertaining how the results will be analyzed and reported.

Program evaluation can be formal or informal. It can be intuitive or analytical. It can be formative and occur periodically throughout the year, or it can be summative and done at one particular time to cover an entire program. Whatever the style or method, program evaluations are useful in identifying key problems, planning and implementing means to address problems and goals, and raising understanding in order to direct efforts.

Evaluation might focus on program goals, outcome measures, or process measures. Program goals are frequently measured by determining if the objectives for a program have been met. For example, an agency might have an organizational objective of recruiting X number of volunteers in appropriate positions. The evaluator would then see if that measurable objective has been attained.

Outcome measures might relate to more qualitative dimensions of what happens to volunteers as a result of their service. Other outcomes to measure might be budget accuracy, funding, training, relationships with other community agencies, public relations, board and committee participation, accomplishments, concerns, information on special projects, cost effectiveness, general program information, and hours expended.

A number of process measures might be evaluated such as the number of volunteer assignments, the time spent by active volunteers, the potential volunteers, the number of days before volunteers are assigned, the number of contacts made to recruit one volunteer, the average duration of volunteer participation, or the hours contributed (Pryor, 1982).

Evaluating the performance of an individual volunteer as an aspect of supervision was discussed earlier. In general, the same process of developing criteria, collecting data, and interpreting data should be used with individual volunteer evaluation. The evaluation should be formative (once every three months, for example) for long-term volunteers and summative for "lend-a-hand" volunteers. The evaluation should include feedback based on the position description and the expectations of the agency. The volunteer should know what the evaluation criteria are from the outset. The supervisor should be as specific as possible about the volunteer's accomplishments and should offer suggestions on how to improve or how to continue to do an effective job. It is useful to keep written notes or evaluation forms on file for future review or in the event the volunteer needs a letter of reference from the supervisor.

The supervisor and other staff ought to be evaluated periodically by the volunteers. This can be in the form of a brief questionnaire or might be a formal part of the conference between the supervisor and the volunteer. Again, the criteria for effective volunteer management should be known by both volunteers and the regular staff person, and evaluation should be based on those criteria. As with volunteers, the staff member needs feedback from his or her supervisor as well as from the volunteers who are being supervised.

In general, evaluation should occur at all levels—volunteer managers should be evaluated by volunteers as well as their supervisors; volunteers should be self-evaluated, evaluated by clients, and evaluated by the paid staff; the program should be evaluated by the board or commission, the staff, the volunteers, and the clientele served. In addition to the people that are involved, various instruments should be used. Information from different perspectives obtained in both qualitative and quantitative forms will be most useful in providing the best possible volunteer program. Appendices P–1 through P–4 provide some examples of possible evaluation instruments.

Recognizing Volunteer Worth

The recognition of volunteers requires open and creative thinking. Recognition involves two basic aspects: (a) letting the volunteer know that she or he is appreciated and worthwhile to the organization, and (b) proving and showing volunteers, the agency, and the community the value of the volunteer program.

Most attempts to document volunteer worth have been underestimations of what really is occurring. It is difficult to depict the true value of voluntary efforts because intrinsic motivations and outcomes are very difficult to measure. It is very difficult to enable a volunteer to realize his or her impact on the larger organization without specific measures of volunteer worth. The onus has been on the agency to demonstrate the worth, but most organizations, including leisure service agencies, have been negligent in measuring much more than time contributed.

The value of a volunteer effort is witnessed by a number of specific groups. For purposes of this discussion, four groups will be identified including the community, the volunteers, the agency, and the clientele served:

1. The group affected by the merit of volunteer programs is the community or the society in general. The community includes both citizens and organizations. Because volunteers are putting forth effort, the quality of life is improved in a community.

2. The volunteers include all who participate in a particular program and are most obviously aware of the value of

volunteering. Their rewards come from something other than a paycheck.

3. The agency also receives much value. The agency itself benefits through the use of volunteers because of the positive public relations that are extended. The staff who work for an agency also receive the benefits of the volunteer program.

4. The clients served may see the benefits of volunteer programs most readily. The participants in an agency's program can be the biggest advocates for the value of using volunteers.

Each of these groups must be continually appraised of how the volunteer program is effective. Each must be acknowledged when assessing the value of the volunteer programs in leisure service organizations.

Exchange theory provides a means for understanding how recognition is created in organizations. Four basic assumptions are offered here which volunteers, the agency, or the community in general may want to consider. First, those who volunteer do so as a means of obtaining desired goals. Second, all activity entails some cost in time, energy, dollars. Third, volunteers, the agency, and the community seek to economize their activities by keeping costs below or equal to the rewards. Fourth, only those volunteer activities that create a profit or have merit across time are continued. This concept applies to all recipient groups that have been identified.

Recognizing Individuals

Probably the most meaningful kind of personal recognition that can be given is to say thank you often and in as many ways as possible. There is no such thing as too much recognition (Kennedy, 1985), and it is not possible to say thank you too many times. Actually stating "thank you" in words is extremely important. It is just plain good communication policy, and it helps people feel they are needed. Praise and recognition are extremely important to everyone. When accomplishments are recognized, people are motivated to continue moving forward. Nonmonetary rewards such as praise and other verbal recognition have been undervalued and underutilized in many agencies. Since volunteers receive no actual pay, recognition is often the currency of exchange.

Many other ways exist for recognizing the worth of volunteers. Recognition amounts to saying thank you in small ways (most of the time), in big splurges (occasionally), often verbally, and sometimes formally. People need to be recognized with signs of appreciation that are significant to them. Here are some examples of formal means:

1. Distribute a "Monday Memo" which identifies the simple things that particular people have done to make things run more smoothly.

2. Use insignia or badges of various kinds to show how many hours people have worked in a particular place.

3. Have a recognition banquet.

4. Give pins, plaques, and other physical items.

5. Hold a surprise party for a dedicated volunteer.

Informal means include a verbal or handwritten thank you, but the most meaningful way to recognize volunteers is to respect them—listen to what they have to say, use their time and talents wisely, reward them for participation and success. Appendix Q shows 101 ways that volunteers can be recognized both formally and informally.

In whatever form, recognition is welcomed when it is genuine, proportionate to the work done, and related to on-the-job activity. Recognition might also refer to additional duties or a new position in the organization.

Recognition cannot stop with volunteers. Staff must also be recognized for their efforts in working with volunteers. By recognizing volunteers, an agency recognizes itself and honors itself. The publicity speaks not only to the volunteer, but to the community as well. Staff can see the important roles they have had to play in bringing about the recognition.

Recognizing Economic Worth

Another way to recognize the value of volunteers is through economic analyses. The key to cost-benefit analysis is creativity, because little consensus exists concerning the best way to analyze costs and benefits with volunteers. No right and wrong ways exist. Cost-benefit analysis as a way of thinking may help staff, agencies, the community, and even the volunteers themselves to understand better the contributions of volunteers.

It is difficult to put costs or benefits into economic terms. Qualitative dimensions frequently do not lend themselves to quantitative terms. The goal of any form of cost-benefit analysis must be to provide the decision maker with more and better information than is otherwise available (Moore, 1978). One of the biggest criticisms of cost-benefit analysis is that benefits are impossible to measure because they are intangible; cost and benefits are incommensurable. The inability to quantify or to find a market value should not, however, preclude analysis.

Benefits are not the same as outputs. For example, an output is easily quantifiable as a unit of work or effort such as number of hours or number of participants. Benefits involve the more qualitative assessment of the participant, which addresses how the program affected them. Some benefits (e.g., increase in staff morale) may simply not be calculable. For these reasons it may be best to stick with cost-effectiveness analyses rather than cost-benefit analysis. A cost-effectiveness analysis is a way of looking at the cost of providing the same benefit in other ways.

Several steps exist in doing a cost-effectiveness analysis (Moore, 1978):

1. Identify the objectives or the criteria for success of the analysis, which must be clearly measurable.

2. Identify the jobs or the activities which exist.

3. Itemize the direct and indirect costs of the program such as coordinator's salary, recordkeeping, secretarial time, plaques and other forms of recognition, mileage, meals, printed materials, manuals, office supplies, insurance, etc., and include the percentage for indirect costs such as overhead, office space, utilities, other staff, record-keeping, equipment use, etc.

4. Establish the outputs (i.e., the total number of hours of volunteer service). If a volunteer coordinator does not know the exact number of hours, a random sample can be conducted to determine this. It is best to keep good records in a system that allows the data to be directly accessed.

5. Calculate the total number of hours of service divided by 2080 (40 hours per week times 52 weeks per year) to arrive at the full-time equivalent (FTE) of volunteer time, and then convert this to a salary. Questions always are raised concerning what the equivalent salary should be. This might be done using the minimum wage or a figure of $4.86 which was established by Wolozin formula (Moore, 1978). The national median wage or the average wage of the agency could be used. Probably the best comparison would be to determine the comparable (equivalent) paid wage. This is done by identifying the tasks and roles, assessing the duties and knowledge, comparing the volunteer to the standard employment classification system, locating the yearly salary and calculating an hourly rate, and multiplying the hourly rate by the number of volunteer hours. Another possibility is to use the salary that a person might get if he or she were working in a regular paid job in that particular area of expertise.

6. Develop a ratio to show that every dollar spent on volunteers yields X dollars of output. This might be thought of as the cost to buy the services (Utterback & Heyman, 1984). It is probably better not to consider this as dollars saved, but to calculate the value of the added services. The value of the volunteer work is not the earning power, but the actual value of the contribution.

Other calculations can be done to assist the coordinator in management decisions. One can calculate the cost per volunteer, the cost per client, and the cost per service hour. See Appendices R and S for a worksheet explaining this economic procedure as well as a short example of the calculation of the value of using volunteer coaches.

SUMMARY

The nuts and bolts of volunteer management include a system of tasks that result in mutual benefits to an agency and to volunteers. The major components of the system involve planning, marketing, training and placement, supervision and recordkeeping, evaluation, and recognition. Each of these components is dependent upon each of the other components. Each is generic to any kind of personnel management, whether for paid staff or volunteers.

Volunteer management is time consuming. Volunteers are not the "free help" they are sometimes perceived to be. A systematic program for working with volunteers can provide many benefits to volunteers, the agency, and the community, but such a program will take time, effort, and support. The tips presented in this chapter should provide food for thought for anyone working with volunteers. It may be impossible to do everything that has been suggested, but the leisure service provider is encouraged to consider what makes the best management sense for the particular agency and for the volunteers and clientele with whom the professional works. Sound techniques of volunteer management will make working with volunteers a satisfying and rewarding opportunity for everyone involved.

4

OTHER CONCERNS RELATED TO VOLUNTEER MANAGEMENT

So far we have discussed the general aspects of operating a volunteer program: planning, marketing, training, supervision, and recognition. Now we explore some of the trends, issues, and special considerations that apply to the utilization of volunteers by leisure service organizations.

VOLUNTEERS AND THE LIABILITY CRISIS

Managers and administrators of leisure service organizations are well aware of the dual threat imposed by the likelihood of a lawsuit brought against the agency and the skyrocketing costs of premiums for liability insurance. To say that we live in a litigious-minded society is indeed an understatement. Attend any type of a professional conference, open any magazine or journal intended for the leisure service field, or talk to any board member or manager on the front line, and the topics of lawsuits and liability insurance are guaranteed to arise.

The effects of this crisis are being manifested in many ways, chief among them the reluctance on the part of many people to continue serving or even consider serving as board members, coaches, or direct-service volunteers in leisure service organizations. In the AALR survey discussed in Chapter 2, the section in which respondents completed open-ended questions revealed a number of comments which indicate that administrators are finding it increasingly more difficult to locate willing volunteers. While time demands certainly can be considered one cause, recent large-scale surveys of persons in volunteer organizations point to the fact that many fear the possibility of a lawsuit resulting from their role as a volunteer. The Gallup Organization (1987) queried 600 leaders (both administrators and board members) of voluntary organizations, and half reported a decline in volunteers which could be linked to liability concerns. Likewise, a Peat, Marwick study (1987) of 2,500 voluntary agency managers concluded that the liability situation had reached the crisis stage.

Who's to blame? Possibilities range from individuals who bring frivolous, costly lawsuits, padded with exorbitant amounts for pain and suffering; to lawyers who are more than ready to litigate such actions; to insurance companies who claim to be victims of circumstance, yet simply pass on costs via triple-digit premium increases; to the recreation and park departments themselves, in failing to adopt strategies to reduce the likelihood of an accident and a resulting lawsuit ever occurring in the first place. Of the respondents to the Peat, Marwick survey (1987), half pointed the finger at lawyers and juries who award huge sums and half said the insurance industry was to blame. Nearly half of the respondents felt that the publicity generated from lawsuits and outrageous settlements helped to fan the flames and keep the cycle going.

As to actual numbers of lawsuits brought against organizations, board members or executives, or individual volunteers, the findings reported by Gallup (1987) and Kahn (1985–86) in a survey of 400 leaders of voluntary agencies seem to indicate that the level of fear being expressed is not in concert with the incidence of suits experienced by agencies. In the Gallup survey, only two percent of respondents had been sued as a result of their role within the organization, five percent of the organizations reported suits related directly to the board of directors, and one-fourth said their organization had been sued at some time in the past. Kahn reported 12 percent of those working for a volunteer program had been involved in a trial, settlement either in or out of court, or a threatened court action; another 11 percent indicated they were aware of other agencies who had experienced any of the above actions. Although the percentage of respondents who indicated involvement in lawsuits is small, it is important to note that the amount of settlements was not reported in the surveys. Few voluntary agencies, municipal recreation and parks departments, or individuals could be expected to recover from a multi-million dollar judgment against them. Thus, the fear of being sued is understandable, even though the incidence of litigation remains low for reporting organizations.

An additional factor gleaned from these recent surveys is the startling increase in insurance premiums. Gallup respondents indicated an average premium increase of 155 percent since 1984; of those sampled by Peat, Marwick, one-third said their insurance rates had risen 300 percent since the last renewal period! Only six percent indicated they had not experienced an increase in insurance premiums in the recent past. One could also speculate that, like private consumers, the agencies and organizations are getting reduced coverage while paying sharply increasing premiums.

It is little wonder, then, that executives and board members or commissioners are in a quandary as to how to react to the liability situation. In the attempt to reduce risk, it appears that a number of tactics are being used. An obvious starting point is to ensure that executives and board members have personal liability insurance. Surprisingly, only two-thirds of the organizations represented in the Gallup survey carried director and board member liability insurance; the percentage in the Peat, Marwick poll was slightly higher at three-fourths. Given the circumstances, however, one would expect that nearly all agencies would carry such policies for their executives and board members.

Other reactions from the board perspective include (from Gallup): 50 percent said they perceive that fewer persons are willing to serve on boards or commissions; 16 percent said they have withheld services due to liability fears; 5 percent have made changes in board structure to lessen the likelihood of liability, including the elimination of committees; and 14 percent said entire programs have been abolished because of pervasive lawsuit fears. Eighty percent of the organizations have a regulation which stipulates who can and cannot speak on behalf of the board, and 70 percent of board members are more careful of what they say or do as a result of their voluntary position. If public and nonprofit organizations are to continue in their present structure of using decision-making bodies comprised of volunteers, it is imperative that techniques be developed which will not only place the organization or department at reduced risk but, in addition, alleviate the ubiquitous concern held by individual board members that they are likely to become involved in a litigious action. Specific recommendations are offered later regarding the management of risks.

THE AGENCY/VOLUNTEER RELATIONSHIP

The legal relationship between volunteers and the organization which they serve is being given scrutiny as a result of lawsuits brought against volunteers who have acted improperly, resulting in client or participant injuries, or as a result of actions brought against agencies when volunteers have been injured or treated improperly. A survey by Kahn (1985–86) of administrators of volunteer programs revealed that legal concerns are a top priority and that a large number of managers (41 percent) felt their knowledge of legal issues was inadequate. It is apparent that those who supervise volunteers must either become knowledgeable about legal matters or know where to turn to obtain answers to questions. The majority of respondents to Kahn's survey indicated they seek legal counsel when not clear on legal issues.

In the first area of liability, injury caused *by* a volunteer, the key issues relate to negligence and cause. Kahn notes definitions of negligence do vary from state to state, but the important factor is that volunteers can be held personally liable if they are found to act in a negligent manner (their actions depart from an appropriate standard of care) which causes injury or harm to a participant. Kahn further stresses that about a dozen recent cases have upheld the concept that organizations are responsible for the actions of their volunteers. He amplifies the agency/volunteer relationship in the following manner:

> This imposition of liability for the acts of volunteers is exactly the same as for salaried workers. It is well established that an employer is liable for the acts of its salaried employees if the necessary conditions are satisfied, and recently courts have been applying this scheme of liability to cases where the worker is an unsalaried volunteer. (p. 30)

Again, one cannot escape the need for risk management approaches in current times. The need is apparent to *systematically* plan and operate the volunteer program using the guidelines and principles outlined in Chapter 3. Proper planning, placement, training, supervision, and evaluation of volunteers will not guarantee freedom from court actions, but will reduce the likelihood of exposure to risk.

The second category for concern is liability for injury *to* a volunteer. The strategies mentioned herein also help to create an environment in which the volunteer feels competent and thereby is able to function safely. Nonetheless, incidences have occurred where negligence was shown to exist on behalf of the agency or organization so that volunteers have received judgments for personal injuries.

Kahn notes another area where volunteers have tested the courts, namely their right to maintain their voluntary status. He concludes that volunteers can be fired. If the situation cannot be resolved in any other fashion and a volunteer's services are terminated, then proper documentation must exist. Discrimination and claims of improper selection and training of volunteers have been noted as potential problem areas. The systems approach as outlined in this book will act as a deterrent to such situations.

LEGISLATIVE ATTEMPTS TO IMPROVE THE EXISTING CLIMATE

As a result of the increasing threat of lawsuits coupled with the need to continue to use the talents of volunteers, legislative attempts have been made, primarily at the state level, to protect in greater measure the welfare of those who charitably offer their services. One notable exception has been the effort at the federal level through House Bill 911, the Volunteer Protection Act, to provide an incentive to states which would ultimately make it more difficult to successfully sue a volunteer. The implications of this legislation are discussed later.

McCurley (1987) conducted an analysis of legislation enacted in 1986 and early 1987 to protect volunteers, and noted that during that period 13 states modified the legal framework affecting suits against volunteers. The basic change has been to shift the definition of negligence to more serious or deliberate actions in order to qualify for a legal action. In essence the minor, frivolous suits brought against the volunteer have been the target, while the opportunity to litigate for serious and wanton acts has remained intact for the potential plaintiff. McCurley (p. 7) has developed four levels along a continuum of fault:

1. *Accident:* Something happened, but there was no fault due to an act or omission on the part of a volunteer.

2. *Simple Negligence:* The volunteer contributed to the wrongdoing, but the action was inadvertent or a small mistake was made.

3. *Wanton or Gross Negligence:* The volunteer was responsible for the wrongdoing in a direct way and the result was serious.

4. *Intentional or Malicious Misconduct:* The volunteer engaged in wrongdoing, knowing it was incorrect—a deliberate act.

Prior to the recent legislative thrusts, "simple negligence" was the qualifying level at which to bring suit, but the states who have altered their laws have pushed the definition to wanton or malicious misconduct. Again, the effect has been to afford protection to those injured, yet make it harder for the plaintiff by requiring that a more serious degree of fault on the part of the volunteer be demonstrated.

Originally two groups, coaches of youth sports teams and those who serve as volunteers on boards, were intended to be the prime beneficiaries of the revised legislation. Some states have also included other volunteers who provide direct service, court-referred volunteers, and organizations or corporations who engage in large-scale charitable projects under the protection available through the more stringent laws. McCurley summarized the new laws as having effects in three ways: volunteers now have to be directly involved in the improper action, with the result that it becomes more difficult to sue a board member; small errors on the part of volunteers should not result in court actions, although volunteers can still be held accountable for serious mistakes; and willful or deliberate acts of a serious nature by a volunteer can result in a legitimate suit. He further emphasized that the new state laws have not prevented volunteers from being sued, nor have they eliminated the need for insurance protection. Furthermore, and perhaps of greatest importance to those reading this book, *it has not eliminated the need for good volunteer management.* One outcome of these legislative initiatives has been that training is now mandated for certain volunteer positions. A case in point is the growth of certification plans for coaches of youth sports. This topic is discussed later in the chapter.

At the federal level, attempts were made by both the 99th and 100th Congress to move a bill forward which would create legislation to afford greater protection to citizen volunteers. Originally introduced in the House by Representative John Porter and followed by a similar bill in the Senate written by John Melcher, the measure was designated as H.R. 911. Attention was drawn to the state of emergency experienced by volunteer administrators and agencies who found it difficult to recruit potential volunteers because of liability concerns. The intent of the bill was to provide an incentive to states to write legislation that would protect individual volunteers from civil liability when performing within the scope of their duties, providing that any damage or injury was not willful on the part of the volunteer. The incentive to states was the withdrawal of one percent of their Social Service Block Grants if they failed to adopt such legislation, with the funds being redistributed to states that had complied.

As expected, support came from numerous nonprofit organizations, but Haberek (1987) noted that grass-roots activity at the local level was proceeding at a slower pace than was necessary. Hearings were held in the Senate during May of 1988, and over 200 co-sponsors backed the measure in the House. However, as the 100th Congress drew to a close in the fall of 1988, it again appeared that no vote would be taken on the floor and the bill would die in committee.

If attempts are to be successful in the future, leisure service agencies must play a prominent role with other charitable, social service organizations. One fact remains clear: the problem will remain until strategies are implemented to deal with the issue. Some have expressed a preference for an approach that would force agencies to pay greater attention to the selection, training, and monitoring of all volunteers, coupled with active risk-management plans. Such tactics will not completely eliminate suits or threatened court actions, but they will bring about a situation whereby volunteers are competent, know how to prevent accidents wherever possible, and know how to respond if an emergency does occur. The preferred option is for leisure service managers to take an aggressive stance in fully preparing volunteers for their duties. Legislation must also be drafted which rejects frivolous nuisance lawsuits. Legislative momentum can be expected to continue at the state level, and if passage of a federal law such as H.R. 911 happens in the near future, the fears of current or prospective volunteers will be reduced.

CURRENT AND FUTURE ROLES FOR VOLUNTEERS

The concluding section of the AALR survey asked participants to examine currently successful roles and possible future roles for volunteers in leisure service organizations. Stated earlier was the idea that external conditions present at any given time affect volunteer participation. Political, social, and economic conditions also greatly affect the roles or tasks in which volunteers engage. Thus, the survey questions in the final section of the AALR Survey allowed a look at the common tasks performed with success, and projected some of the ways that agencies could benefit through new or expanded use of volunteers. For ease in presentation, the tasks or roles are discussed from top to bottom in terms of rankings (numbers given in parentheses represent raw figures, not percentages from the survey). Individual responses from the survey instrument were categorized so that topical areas could be discussed.

Not surprisingly, AALR members (69) listed leading or assisting with an activity or program as the area in which volunteers were currently most successful. Coaching or assisting with sports (30) and helping with special events (30) followed as other areas of success. Respondents from AALR noted participation on boards or commissions (12) as a category of effectiveness, and other roles included: assisting with the operational or supervisory aspects of a recreational facility (10), helping out with office work (5), fund raising (4), and officiating (2). A variety of other functions which tallied only a single response included: phone chairperson, neighborhood park supervisor, information giver, junior counselor, and chaplain's assistant. It is clear that the scope of duties performed by leisure service volunteers extends beyond the apparent ones of leading an activity or coaching.

These AALR findings are comparable to a survey conducted by Allen, Kraus, and Williams-Andy (1986) of the Philadelphia Recreation Department and Fairmount Park. Volunteers were found most often to work with special events, serve as leaders or advisors to athletic organizations, lead activities themselves, or help with fund raising. Administrative assistance, such as registering or clerical work, was also seen as appropriate for volunteers. Neighborhood projects, i.e., clean-up days or providing specialized services, were noted as well.

Future Roles

When AALR members were given the opportunity to suggest new roles for volunteers, many of the same types of jobs were listed, but the emphasis (in terms of priority) shifted somewhat as compared to current roles. Activity assistance (34) was mentioned most often as a desired future role. Although the role itself is not novel, the variety of specific activities given was quite large. Survey participants definitely perceived a continued role for volunteers in directly leading or supporting the conduct of activity programs.

The next most popular response from the survey was fund raising (10). Perhaps it is the sociopolitical characteristic of constrained budgets for those providing leisure opportunities which elevated fund raising as a desired role for volunteers in the future. Concessions planning and work with booster clubs were given as specific functions. As the fund-raising function becomes increasingly more sophisticated, this may indeed become an area where leisure services may benefit through the use of knowledgeable volunteers.

Following fund raising as a future task for volunteers were the categories of facility assistance (9) and office or clerical work

(8). Other, less frequently given answers which could be grouped were: coaching sports, committee or board membership, officiating, and special event aid. Unique responses (listed only once) suggested many interesting potential volunteer roles: video assistant, public relations specialist, project evaluator, staff trainer, and remotivation therapist were among this group. Those who participated in the survey were not at a loss when thinking about ways that volunteers could be utilized.

Another category, mentioned by nine persons, was the development or improvement of the volunteer program by using volunteer talent. One suggestion was a volunteer who would serve in the capacity of volunteer coordinator. Recruiting other volunteers was noted as an appropriate activity for current volunteers. Others hinted that operational or management aspects of the volunteer program could be handled by volunteers themselves.

The intent of this open-response exercise was not to develop a definitive list of potential volunteer roles and then construct a national recruiting plan for such specialists. Rather, it was thought that an interesting comparison could be made between currently successful roles occupied by volunteers and the desired or future ones. It should also be stressed that many, many examples exist across the country where volunteers have more than proven their worth in outdoor or environmental projects, in instituting fund raising projects, and in helping out whenever a need has arisen. A few of these notable success stories involving volunteers are highlighted in the following paragraphs.

One recent endeavor which drew national attention was the National Volunteer Project under the direction of the Appalachian Mountain Club (see Rawls, 1983; Moore, La Forge, & Martorelli, 1987). A grant was obtained from the Richard King Mellon Foundation in Pittsburgh, and six demonstration projects were completed in New Mexico, Washington State, Florida, California, Pennsylvania, and Colorado. The projects included trail maintenance and construction, sign repair, innovative ways to attract other volunteers, education efforts aimed at providing a more knowledgeable outdoor user, resource studies, and other land management projects. One notable example from the project was the cooperation gained from the U.S. Forest Service whereby specialists were assigned to work on a full-time basis with the Appalachian Mountain Club. This type of cooperative agreement best illustrates the concept of "partnerships."

The U.S. Forest Service and the National Park Service both have longstanding, organized volunteer programs (Greer, 1985). The Forest Service has used the talents of volunteers since its inception in 1905, and in 1972 the Volunteers in the National Forests Act permitted an expansion of their use. Typical areas of service have been trail maintenance, mapping work and publications, camp hosts, and general maintenance work. Help has also been given in data collection regarding site use or wildlife counts. The companion program in the National Park Service is the Volunteers in the Park Program, wherein volunteers provide assistance in interpretation and information dissemination as well as with the traditional office work and maintenance duties. A cooperative program with Camp Fire, Inc., was established where high school youth were chosen to perform a number of ecological service projects in selected national parks (Henderer, 1983). Both the Forest Service and Park Service have benefitted through a systematic approach to recruiting, training, and managing of volunteers.

Volunteer talents have been put to use in a number of research projects at federal or state sites. Magyar (1983) noted the important role played by volunteers in caring for endangered species and in projects such as bird banding and counting. Such work has often fueled a professional interest for students who have participated. Other research efforts have been aided by volunteers who record head counts, work in data preparation or tabulation, and help to prepare reports of the completed research.

States have also become increasingly more sophisticated in their marketing orientations to potential volunteers. Most states now have a coordinated effort, either in a centralized or decentralized fashion, to attract volunteers. Various green thumb or volunteer-in-the-park programs operate at the state level. New York (O'Brien, 1983) has reported success in using volunteers to recreate history through serving as docents dressed in period costume. Village persons, craftsmen, and soldiers are typical roles portrayed by volunteers with an interest in living history. Trail maintenance, building rehabilitation, and program leadership are functions performed by volunteers working in state parks. The sophistication has also extended to management aspects as well. For example, Pennsylvania's Volunteers In Parks Act (*Volunteers in Parks*, 1982) affords volunteers liability protection, auto insurance coverage if driving is designated under the tasks performed as an official volunteer, and entitlement to protection under worker's compensation. With state park budgets under continued scrutiny, it would be reasonable to assume that volunteers will be valued as an important component to complement what is often an understaffed workforce.

Creativity at the municipal or community level of government has also been evident in conceiving, implementing, and completing tasks which could not be undertaken by full-time leisure services staff alone. The Philadelphia Recreation Volunteerism Project, funded through the National Recreation Foundation and the Fels Foundation, provided incentives to local communities to develop innovative volunteer projects (Allen, Kraus, & Williams-Andy, 1986). The outcome of these efforts resulted in effectiveness in four areas: leadership or leadership training; administrative assistance, including the strengthening of advisory bodies; special events; and maintenance projects. Notable successes included: programs for latch-key children, the integration of handicapped youth in ice-skating programs, a festival to encourage Hispanic pride, and construction of storage space for an indoor facility. The project served to highlight an important point: with the impetus provided through a small amount of seed money and an organized effort on the part of staff, much can be accomplished at the local level when volunteer talent is properly harnessed.

Other municipal projects noted in the literature have been citizens serving as volunteer park rangers through a type of neighborhood watch program in nearby parks (Price, 1984), construction of a nocturnal habitat for animals (Trudeau, 1983), and the development of a gifts catalogue (Migliazzo, 1983) in Westminster, California, where the public is urged to donate money or volunteer talent to help the recreation department. Gaining enthusiasm in many areas is the adopt-a-park concept whereby maintenance activities are done by citizens or financial support is generated by citizens to help pay for park improvements.

The initiation of volunteer support does not always begin with local government officials. There are many examples of beneficial partnerships or projects initiated by the private or corporate sector. Donald Trump's action-oriented approach in marshalling private resources to complete the refurbishing of the Wohlman Rink in Central Park is illustrative of such private sector involvement. Another private concern, Robert Leathers and Associates in Ithaca, New York, has capitalized on the spirit of volunteerism in planning and constructing some 450 playgrounds in 35 states across the country. The Leathers organization provides the technical expertise and allows community volunteers to plan and construct the large, multistation playscapes. Construction of the project resembles a barn-raising of yesteryear, with committee volunteers busy cutting and hauling wood, preparing food, and keeping overeager kids out of the way. The concept is one which brings out the best in private-public cooperation.

The intent has not been to report each instance of novel volunteer use within the nation; space precludes such an exhaustive task. However, the examples given do serve to portray what can be done when vision, creativity, and organizational support are teamed with volunteers who are willing to aid projects in our park and recreation sites. No doubt the future will bring new ventures, and the projections from the AALR respondents give us something to consider. While every community does not have a Donald Trump waiting in the wings, most communities could benefit through volunteers who would help plan and carry out a fundraising project. A need to better supervise volunteer activities was evident from the survey; staff should look to volunteers to help in this regard. It would also appear that special projects would hold appeal for volunteers, e.g., cleaning the stream in a nearby park or helping to build a concession stand that one's children will enjoy. Such projects have a definite beginning and ending, and the results can be easily viewed—aspects that appeal to volunteers.

Many leisure service agencies continually complain that a lack of time precludes the initiation of any type of research, even of an applied nature. Local administrators may wish to consider the example noted above where volunteers assist with projects involving wildlife or endangered species, and attempt to locate persons who are willing to help with research. Program evaluation, market analysis, the collection of data for master planning, historical research—all are potential projects which could be assisted by community volunteers. With creativity and a desire to accomplish a task, the forward-looking administrator will discover exciting ways to use volunteer talent.

SPECIAL GROUPS OF VOLUNTEERS

A number of special groups of volunteers were identified in Chapter 3 in the discussion pertaining to recruitment. An elaboration of the potential benefits to the leisure service agency and the special volunteers themselves is provided in this section. Unique strategies may be necessary in some cases to market volunteerism to these groups; in other cases, the same management techniques used for any volunteer are applicable. These special groups include: older adults; persons with disabilities, who often reside in the community in group homes or other congregate living arrangements; court-referred volunteers; and children.

Older Adults

Two important notions are apparent when considering older adults as volunteers. The first is that the older population is growing (now about 12 percent of the total population), and the second is that most surveys reveal the fact that this group is currently underutilized as a volunteer source. Administrators of leisure programs should also be aware that the segment containing the eldest of the older adults—those above age 75—is growing at a faster rate than is the population of persons 65 and older. Thus, it is likely that many older persons reside in every community.

It was mentioned earlier that volunteering appears to taper off among older persons as compared to the under-65 population. However, there is not complete agreement on this point in the empirical literature. Exact numbers cited of older volunteers do vary according to source and how volunteerism is defined. A recent Gallup Poll (1986) defining involvement in charitable or social service activities noted that 44 percent of persons age 65 and over are serving in such capacities, a figure slightly above that group's total population percentage of 36 percent. Involvement for the over-65 age group was actually higher than either the 50–64 age group or the total 50-and-over group. The Gallup National Survey conducted in 1985 used a broader definition of volunteer activities, and volunteering declined with each age group of adults examined. The national average was roughly 50 percent, while those ages 50–64 reported a 44 percent rate, those ages 65–74 reported a 43 percent rate, and the oldest, over age 75, noted a 25 percent rate of participation. The United Media Enterprises (1983) found the over-65 population to volunteer at a 38 percent rate, below the norm for all groups (46 percent). In fact, the over-65 population reported the lowest level of volunteering for any of the eight age groups examined. Harris's Survey (1981) noted that 23 percent of adults over age 65 volunteer, with older men volunteering at a slightly higher rate than in an earlier study, and older blacks volunteering at a slightly lower rate than older whites. It is evident that such studies are not in agreement as to the percent of the aging population that elects to volunteer.

Another finding revealed in these national surveys is that a number of older adults desire to volunteer or see themselves as a potential volunteer, yet for one reason or another are not doing so. About ten percent in the 1981 Harris poll said they desired to volunteer but weren't doing so. McGuire and Adams (1986) investigated older volunteers in outdoor recreation sites and found that about 16 percent said they could teach an outdoor activity or skill, but three-fourths of that group weren't doing so. The reasons for this were: not knowing the right person or agency to contact; not having enough personal time; health reasons; and not having been asked by anyone. Other reasons for nonparticipation which Harris (1975) found included: lack of transportation; other family responsibilities; being too busy with work; and lack of energy. What is interesting to note is that many older respondents do not perceive themselves as having considerable free time; in fact, to the contrary, while most have disengaged from the workforce, they are involved in a number of activities and often find competing activities or desires to be a problem. Thus, a recruiting effort which perceives older adults as idle with vast blocks of unscheduled time may be in error.

On a very practical plane or one oriented to personal benefit, there are many reasons to justify seeking out and involving older adults. Theories of aging often speak about the continued process of role replacement or substitution as one ages. Parallels can be drawn between the positive benefits from the work setting—e.g., accomplishing tasks, working with a group, personal creativity—and similar benefits which can be realized from volunteer endeavors during retirement. Older volunteers in various settings have reported the same types of benefits from their service as have persons from younger age groups. The relative value or priority may shift, depending on life circumstances (perhaps a need for social contact arises after the loss of a close friend), but the benefits apparent to older volunteers match those to be gained by any volunteer.

Leisure service administrators should carefully consider the tasks to which older volunteers can bring particular expertise or talent. Any teaching, leading, skill-building, counseling, or facilitating role may be appropriate for an older volunteer if it matches his or her interests and capabilities. MacNeil and Teague (1987) have noted recreation agencies as successful in using older volunteers in roles such as playing music, performing maintenance tasks, and constructing and repairing toys, as well as the active administration of the Retired Senior Volunteer Program under the auspices of the municipal leisure services department. Other possible projects could include: assistance with the interpretation of local history, as in the living history concept; intergenerational efforts, where all ages come together for community benefit; senior clubs who band together to assist with a large, community-wide event; and assuming nurturing roles in after-school or latch-key programs. The possibilities are endless, and older volunteers themselves may provide excellent feedback in exploring further ways that they can offer assistance.

An approach focused on reaching, enlisting, and supporting older volunteers should include the following:

- The message must be delivered that older volunteers are encouraged to link with the leisure services organization. There is a consensus that many over-65 persons are willing to volunteer, but need to be matched with the correct person or agency representative. The information and referral function is critical if older adults are to become volunteers.

- Don't make the hasty generalization that the elderly are sitting at home with nothing to do. Many of them express time constraints, and idleness is far from a reality. Scheduling will be an important consideration for this group, just as it is for others.

- A one-to-one approach may be necessary to coax the reluctant older volunteer. Granted, this may take time, but personal attention may be the answer to reaching the hesitant volunteer.

- Group approaches can also prove very successful. Often a specific project—park beautification efforts, fund raisers with an immediate goal, or time-bound, urgent problem solvers, as examples—can mobilize support through clubs or centers.

- Discover why the older adult wishes to volunteer. Don't assume all retired individuals are lonely. Tedrick (1975) found the social benefit to be a relatively low priority for foster grandparents and retired senior volunteers.

- Don't forget to evaluate and provide feedback to older volunteers. Like any volunteer, they have a keen desire to know the impact of their efforts.

With certain modifications or shifted emphasis, the same management techniques outlined in Chapter 3 will be successful with older adults. It is apparent that this is one group that can be encouraged to volunteer, and one whose members will greatly benefit through expanded service.

Persons with Disabilities

One societal trend which has direct implication for the recruitment of special volunteer groups is the process of deinstitutionalization of persons with disabilities which has occurred at a swift pace over the past few years. With the philosophy of "least restrictive environment" in mind, many large state institutions began a process of seeking appropriate community residences for persons who previously had not been considered candidates for noninstitutional living. Persons with mental retardation or developmental disabilities who are at a higher level of functioning have been prime candidates for community placement. Congregate housing arrangements and other forms of community living residences are now common in nearly all cities, towns, and villages.

Both the age span and the types of disabilities represented by those who reside in community locales are factors which must be considered when such individuals are viewed as potential volunteers. Two points are evident: the number of persons with disabilities who live outside of an institutional environment is significant and will not likely decrease, and the benefits to be gained by volunteering could be particularly meaningful for this group. While some of these persons find a structure to the day through participation in community workshops or supervised employment experiences, there is often a lack of leisure time opportunities. Thus, volunteering could offer a person with special needs an appropriate way to structure free time and build self-esteem through the accomplishment of volunteer goals or tasks.

Shank (1984) noted that very few disabled persons are employed in leisure service organizations. He cited a national study conducted in the early 1970s which indicated that approximately one percent of leisure service employees had a disability, and the vast majority of those were utilized in non-professional capacities. A follow-up study was done to determine barriers to employment of such persons in leisure service agencies. Identified as barriers were unfavorable attitudes on the part of employees, problems created by the nature of the physical disability, poor career guidance materials (many persons with disabilities weren't aware of leisure as a career field), and demands inherent in the provision of recreation activities which made participation difficult for persons with disabilities (but perhaps only an active, teaching or leading role was considered here). These barriers would logically need to be considered if volunteering rather than work were the area of focus.

In a similar vein, Kennedy, Austin, and Smith (1987) have given a comprehensive discussion of the barriers which can block people with special needs from participating in recreation activities. Three broad categories were classified as intrinsic, environmental, and communication barriers. Intrinsic barriers include a lack of knowledge about programs and services; social ineffectiveness, perhaps stemming from parental overprotection or lack of practice in social situations due to the living situation; health problems associated with a disease or disability which may prevent one from participating in certain activities; physical or psychological dependency, which can be an artifact of a system which forces one to become dependent; and skill gaps, where not knowing how to do something prevents one from engaging in an opportunity. Environmental constraints include attitudinal barriers manifested in overt negative behaviors toward a person with disabilities, or paternalistic or simply apathetic behavior toward those with special needs. Other environmental problems can be architectural (steps, no ramps) or ecological (snow, rain). Communication barriers include not knowing how to communicate, not making the effort to learn assistive communication methods, or simply not knowing how to contact persons with disabilities. If efforts to reach potential volunteers with disabilities are to be successful, such barriers must be identified and overcome.

With the preceding discussion as a background, the following suggestions are offered in utilizing the talents of persons with disabilities who live within the community. Administrators or managers will need to create a plan aimed at identifying residents with special needs. Appropriate agencies and local planning bodies would be a good starting place. Ideally, the leisure service organization should be active in gathering this information for the purpose of including such individuals in regularly scheduled recreational events. If this is not the case, then the first task at hand is locating potential volunteers among persons who have disabilities.

Plan to spend an adequate amount of time to ensure that the match between the special volunteer and the task to be completed is a sound one. For persons with physical disabilities, there are certainly many jobs which can be done irrespective of mobility—fund raising, teaching various skills, and special events planning. Persons with developmental disabilities may serve as volunteers in routine tasks, as aides in activity settings, or as helpers in ecological projects. An up-to-date file of volunteer descriptions will prove invaluable.

Be aware that activity modification can apply to volunteer

tasks just as it can to recreation participation. Examine what key elements are needed to complete a job. If the volunteer does not possess the ability to do the entire task, consider breaking it down into component parts. Most complex tasks can be simplified. Two or three volunteers with disabilities can be used to do a job which might normally be completed by one person. Don't consider special volunteers only from the perspective of what can't be done. They bring special talents just as do any other types of volunteers.

If your staff is a victim of any of the attitudinal barriers previously discussed, plan to do some education. The worst possible situation would be one of an eager volunteer with a disability who is shown apathy or paternalism on the part of the leisure services employee. An appropriate match is needed not only in terms of the volunteer and the task to be accomplished, but also in terms of the staff person who will give the volunteer guidance and supervision.

Time must be taken to determine any barriers which may be experienced by the volunteer with special needs. Scheduling and means of transportation must be carefully coordinated. Remember that snow, rain, or other weather-related problems often create particular hurdles for those with gait or mobility deficiencies. If unique accessibility problems exist at a given volunteer site, they must be attended to. During the interview stage, all potential barriers should be discussed with the prospective volunteer. It is imperative that the agency be forthright in detailing accommodations that may be necessary to allow the volunteer access to the facility and to permit successful completion of the task assigned.

Should skills (social or task-oriented) be lacking in volunteers with disabling conditions, be prepared to teach or educate. Training is an established part of the volunteer management system, and special volunteers can require minimal or extensive amounts depending upon the tasks to be undertaken. Special approaches to training may be required as well. Attention to method of communication, organization and breakdown of learning tasks, rate of progression, and opportunity for hands-on, experiential training will be factors to be considered when designing training sessions. An educator who has experience with the particular disability under consideration may be sought as a volunteer. Training for the special volunteer is similar to all aspects of the volunteer management system—it requires planning, time, and agency effort to reach the desired goals.

Leisure service organizations must be in the forefront in encouraging persons with disabilities to become volunteers. A humanistic field cannot afford to claim scheduling problems, or lack of staff capabilities, or sentiments of "it's not our primary purpose" as reasons to overlook volunteers who may have special needs but would ultimately benefit greatly through their service. Helping others, sharing talents, and improving lives are benefits all volunteers can experience. A boost in self-esteem is a significant reward to the special volunteer desiring to assist others.

Volunteers from the Court System

One could legitimately question the philosophical happenstance of court-referred "volunteers" who are assigned to fulfill obligations of a specified length of community service. While not volunteers in a pure sense, most cities and counties are increasingly using alternative sentencing as a method of dealing with overcrowding of detention facilities. It is likely that parks departments and recreation agencies may qualify to receive those who have been assigned such alternative sentences. The situation is somewhat unique from the perspective of volunteer management.

Ellis (1986, pp. 98–99) has noted a number of policy implications pertaining to court-assigned volunteers. The agency should have a clear idea of the minimum number of hours to be served if such volunteers are to be accepted. If the tasks to be done require little planning or training, the amount of time served may be irrelevant. If the tasks require more than minimal training and organization, however, a group of persons with few hours to serve may not suit the agency's needs.

The department might also stipulate that information be given on the nature and purpose of the alternative sentence. Prudence demands caution in using volunteers who must submit to community service. There are projects that certainly do lend themselves to short-term, intensive workers who do not need high levels of training or skill. Clean-up details or other maintenance projects may be ideal. Like all other situations, the match between the volunteer and the task to be undertaken is critical.

Ellis (1986) also indicates that the agency must decide beforehand how to deal with court-assigned persons who don't fulfill their obligation. Is the court or a probation officer to be notified? These issues must be carefully considered.

It is likely that the practice of alternative sentencing will continue in the future. While an opportunity exists for leisure service organizations to utilize persons referred from the court system, the advantages must be weighed against the effort required to properly place, assign, and monitor those assigned to community service. Projects can be identified where the benefits undoubtedly surpass the agency's costs. Agencies considering the use of court-referred "volunteers" are advised to contact local agencies which have experience with such workers to gain an understanding of the positive and negative factors associated with their utilization.

Children as Volunteers

Another special group for leisure service organizations to consider as volunteers is children. Volunteering can present unique benefits to kids, among them the increased self-esteem that arises from being viewed as a contributor rather than just a recipient of services or programs. Another apparent reward for volunteering is that children will gain directly from their labors—painting a room or lounge at a center or cleaning up a park in their neighborhood are examples. The following discussion does not detail all of the principles of volunteering or volunteer management; such an examination is provided in Chapter 3. However, there are certain considerations that should be noted if leisure service departments are to actively recruit and use youthful volunteers.

One possible value of volunteering which has been considered recently (see Goode, 1988) by child development specialists, the clergy, and others concerned with the proper upbringing of our children is its link to instilling a sense of social or moral responsibility. Volunteering offers an excellent and very practical opportunity for children to understand that they can make a contribution to society. Service activities related to park or recreation concerns can provide to children the beginning of what may become a lifelong interest in assisting others, the local community, or the environment in which they live. Young children often are aware of, but feel at a loss in personally dealing with, some of the major social problems or inequities in the world in which they live. The opportunity to assist others can be realized through projects undertaken by or coordinated through leisure service organizations. By being active in such activities as clean-up days, park beautification projects, and painting or maintenance projects, children are able to see that they can make a difference.

Another direct benefit of volunteering for children is that they often can appreciate the results of their labors through re-creating at the site they helped to improve. Many athletic organizations ask for volunteers to help prepare fields prior to the opening of the season. Cutting grass, painting fences or dugouts, and picking up trash are common activities. Youth centers often ask their participants to help paint, volunteer for fund-raising projects, or make telephone calls to gather support for a program. In all of these ventures, the youthful volunteer is able to receive direct benefit from his or her efforts.

Volunteering with a local leisure service agency also allows preteens to discover that there are many roles to be enjoyed with any activity, sport, or event. One does not have to be the "star" or the outstanding player to receive enjoyment. Helping younger children learn to play a sport can be gratifying and lead to a lifelong interest in this area. Many local theater buffs got their start early in life as volunteers who helped to paint scenery, prepare the stage, or make posters. Volunteering offers many ways to learn that there be a number of interesting and worthwhile roles associated with any endeavor.

Volunteering also coincides with the goals of youth organizations who have a service ethic. Parks or recreation departments should capitalize on this opportunity. Many of these organizations, like the Scouts or 4-H Clubs, also have a sincere interest in the environment and outdoor preservation. Often, with a little effort in planning and scheduling, a service project can enlist many of these youth agencies for community betterment. Earth day or other similar conservation projects are natural projects for youth-serving agencies, conservation groups, and school-related clubs.

Another possible benefit to be realized from using youth volunteers is a decrease in the generation gap when parents or other adults join children in a project of shared concern and effort (Ellis, 1983). Getting adults and children together to accomplish a task fosters communication between them and allows them to share equally in the satisfaction of completing the job. Fund-raising projects or undertaking a community needs assessment could be examples where support from volunteers of any age would be needed. The planning should be structured to allow active input by children. This will not only permit them to feel that they are part of a team but, will also provide a perspective that differs from adults.

In conducting group interviews with children aged 5–14, Ellis (1983) obtained their views on volunteering and the role they could play. Their descriptions of volunteering and the benefits to be gained were not markedly different from those of adults. A volunteer was described as one who helps or serves or gives assistance. They described how they felt when volunteering as being satisfied, feeling proud, showing love, and having a sense of accomplishment. When asked what types of volunteer projects they would be willing to do, a number of the responses reflected an interest in ecological or outdoor concerns. Clean-up details were frequently mentioned with parks, ponds, streams, or one's neighborhood as prime sites. Other answers included cleaning up graffiti, teaching people not to litter, preventing fires, and collecting cans. These responses should be of interest to leisure service personnel, as there appears to be an awareness among the youth surveyed of the value of a clean environment. Such interest needs to be translated into active, ongoing projects.

Managers or administrators should employ the same techniques in recruiting, orienting, and placing young volunteers as they would with other groups, although an emphasis on certain areas—training, for example—may be needed. The recruitment of youth should involve the existing group structures available. Church youth groups, Scouts, youth clubs, conservation organizations for children, school affiliated clubs, and all youth athletic associations are prime resources for recruiting. This approach may prove more beneficial than seeking individual youth. Projects suited for such groups also need to be considered. The environmental beautification efforts mentioned are most suitable for group efforts. Certainly teams and athletic associations who use park facilities should be targeted for such improvement projects. A primary role that should be played by the leisure service agency is one of coordination; direction may be needed to mobilize a number of youth organizations and begin the planning effort for a large-scale community project.

Do remember to allow young volunteers to provide ideas on how to complete a task. Ellis (1983) notes this as crucial in working with younger volunteers. If the agency is willing to use their talents, it should be willing to carefully listen to their suggestions.

Special attention must be given to scheduling when children are involved. Obviously, very long stretches of involvement may be inappropriate for younger volunteers. Projects that have a definite beginning and ending and allow the youthful volunteer to see results quickly often work best.

Involve parents in all stages of a project in which their children will be volunteering. A permission slip and a signed contract are recommended. Stressing the benefits of the volunteer effort that will be seen by their children is a good method of selling any project to parents.

Training is certainly a concern when children are serving as volunteers. Previously it was mentioned that a well-run volunteer system is not without its costs. Training represents a cost in human resources. If the amount of time it takes to train a group of children exceeds the projected value of the project, then perhaps a different type of volunteer would be more appropriate. There are many projects, however, which don't require large amounts of training. Beautification often starts simply with picking up trash.

Finally, remember that kids are just like adults in appreciating recognition of their efforts. A button or patch that can be worn on a jacket or bag can be a constant reminder of one's time spent with a volunteer project. The leisure service agency should also be in a position to offer volunteers reduced rates for any activity where a fee is charged. These little incentives or reminders can be most meaningful to children. Anyone who doubts this should consider how many two-inch trophies still remain on children's shelves even though parts are missing and mom or dad has tried to dispose of these keepsakes for years.

It might be fair to conclude that children are often overlooked as a volunteer source. The benefits to be gained through their use as volunteers in leisure service agencies are many. Positive experiences may set the stage for a lifetime of similar activity. When groups of young volunteers are properly directed, their accomplishments can indeed be very significant. Like the other special categories of volunteers in this section, it is recommended that children be considered as a group who will bring much to the volunteer setting within leisure service organizations.

VOLUNTEERS WHO COACH YOUTH SPORTS

It is probably accurate to state that leisure service agencies would be devoid of youth sports programs were it not for the dedicated volunteer administrators, managers, and coaches who combine a love of a particular sport with the desire to share that love with young athletes. However, as indicated previously, the situation is more complex today than it once was. Lawsuits or threatened litigation have created a cloud of negativism which has dampened the desire of both experienced and prospective volunteer coaches. Many volunteer coaches have made the decision to continue in their role, but have done so with a degree of hesitation. Leisure service administrators and the volunteer parent officials of athletic leagues have been left to solve a difficult dilemma—how to maintain what they believe to be worthwhile athletic opportunities for the youth of their communities while providing a climate that is safe for participants and minimizes liability fears. No easy task, indeed, and like private consumers, leagues have found their coffers being emptied to pay for rapidly rising insurance costs.

One obvious approach to alleviate the situation described above has been the development of training programs to educate volunteer coaches about much more than simply the strategy of the game they teach. While at one time training for volunteer coaches may have entailed a hastily organized, one-and-a-half or two-hour session where practice drills were taught, the trend now is for a much more comprehensive format where philosophy, skill development, injury prevention, parental communication, and psychological motivation are covered in a series of highly organized exercises using techniques of group interaction and the latest in multimedia presentations. In the past, training was considered desirable and encouraged, but today safety, liability, and insurance concerns have created a climate where frequently the volunteer coach is required to undergo some form of specific training, often with certification awarded upon completion. Feigley's (1988a, b) analysis of state civil immunity legislation regarding volunteer coaches found two states, New Jersey and New Hampshire, mandating an approved coaches' training workshop with certification in order for the volunteer to quality for civil immunity protection. Where not required by law, many communities have seen the wisdom in such a risk-avoidance approach and have made training programs available or required for all volunteer coaches of children's sports.

Two national programs, the National Youth Sports Coaches Association[1] and the American Coaching Effectiveness Program,[2] have been active in providing comprehensive training for volunteer coaches of youth athletic programs across the nation. The ACEP has estimated that approximately 60,000 coaches have received training through their efforts. Differences do exist in certain areas of focus between the two organizations, but they are similar in that they are national in scope, offer several levels of training, have comprehensive curricula offering instructional units in many areas, use a multimedia approach, and are concerned with certifying local instructors who can then begin training volunteer coaches in their own communities.

As mentioned earlier, the intent of the training far exceeds game- or sport-specific strategy. Those who undergo such training are required to consider some of the fundamental issues confronting a youth coach, such as: "What is my primary goal in undertaking this coaching assignment?" and "How should I balance competitive urges with a philosophy of fun and enjoyment

[1] 2611 Old Okechobee Rd., West Palm Beach, FL 33409
[2] Box 5076, Champaign, IL 61820

for the youthful participants?" Other topics discussed include organizing a well-run practice, safety and the prevention of injuries, how to respond to an accident, teaching sport skills, how to deal with parents, and the psychology of working with young athletes. More specific training and higher level concerns are addressed in leadership sessions for more advanced coaches. Typically, the time required for the workshop is one full day or two half-day sessions, with participants required to do follow-up study on their own. Role playing is often utilized to personalize the instruction.

Not only are such formal training programs available from sources with a national interest, but states have also begun to organize and to teach coaching skills for those within their borders. Some have done so as an outgrowth of legislation aimed to protect volunteer coaches, while at the same time attempting to upgrade their coaching skills. New Jersey's Youth Sports Research Council and Michigan's Youth Sports Institute (see Feigley, 1988a, b) and New York's Volunteer Coaches Institute (see Tedrick & Wagoner, 1985) are examples.

Whether or not certification of coaches is mandatory by state legislation, it is clearly an issue of concern to all parents, public officials, and leisure service administrators, and the wisdom of providing a comprehensive, organized, and effective training program for volunteer youth coaches is readily apparent. Reducing risks and preventing injuries are two critical goals of such formalized training. Having coaches on the field or court who are dedicated to accomplishing these goals is a situation all will heartily support.

The intent of this section has not been to instruct the reader on how to conduct a training program for volunteer coaches; there are many excellent formats available which provide ample detail. Persons who work with athletic leagues for children and teens should be aware, however, that resources are available to assist in the preparation of qualified volunteer managers and coaches. One can turn to organizations such as the National Youth Sports Coaches Association or the American Coaching Effectiveness Program for help in developing a plan for training local coaches. State or regional organizations are other logical resources. It would be a mistake for leisure service managers to avoid volunteer coach training with the thought that time does not permit the organization of a program. Effective help is available and it should be utilized.

Another issue which may arise is the consideration that volunteer coaches are like everyone today in having many commitments and only a lilmited amount of free time. To ask coaches to give up an additional half day or full day to undertake such training might appear to be an unreasonable request. However, the administrator should consider whether he or she can afford *not* to request them to do so. The risks are too great for administrators not to demand training. The coaches themselves wish to feel competent in handling an emergency or injury situation or in dealing with a difficult parent or athlete. Thus, while empathizing with volunteers and their busy schedules, the administrator should nevertheless require and provide appropriate training.

Volunteer training can also offer an appropriate format for dealing with an issue which is often considered a thorn in everyone's side: the much publicized claim that leagues are overly competitive and have a "win at all costs" philosophy that is detrimental to youth. At times, leisure service administrators are among the loudest complainers about such programs, yet often they become willing accomplices by turning over virtually all administrative control to a group of overly zealous parents who feel winning is the primary, perhaps even the only, goal of any athletic endeavor. In such situations, the leisure service organization becomes little more than a maintainer of athletic fields. The point is that training workshops for volunteer coaches offer excellent opportunities to communicate major goals and dictate the level of competitive pressure to be permitted in a league. If administrators feel that competition is reaching a point where fun and skill development are being pushed to the background, then training sessions conducted prior to league play are opportunities to deal with the issue in a straightforward manner. It does appear that a combined effort consisting of the professional view (the paid leisure service administrator) and the lay or parental perspective (those who volunteer to coordinate, coach, and officiate youth sports leagues) can create a philosophy which allows both a reasonable amount of competition and a rewarding, growth-producing experience for the youthful sport enthusiast.

Two final benefits of proper training for volunteer coaches are worthy of note. Leagues may obtain a slightly reduced insurance premium for participants if coaches have attended and successfully completed designated clinics. Over 400 recreation commissions have taken advantage of personal liability insurance which includes coverage for volunteer coaches through a plan promoted through the National Recreation and Park Association[3]. Some organizations, the National Youth Sports Coaches Association, for example, offer liability protection for coaches as an incentive to participate in their training programs. However, the most important benefit to be gained through the training of volunteer coaches is the likelihood that the kids who play in youth sports will receive a richer experience. Since this goal is at the foundation of what coaches are attempting to create, the time and effort devoted to instructional clinics for volunteer coaches is a necessary and valuable expenditure.

BOARDS AND COMMISSIONS

Board and commission members are a special type of volunteer, and many of the principles that apply to other volunteers also apply to them. Their commitment is voluntary, yet, they are unique in their policy-making role. Hence, several aspects of working with these elected or appointed volunteers are noteworthy.

The board of a public or quasi-public recreation, park, or leisure service organization is responsible and accountable. By law, several board functions are mandated. A board is an active and responsible governing body, serving without compensation, holding regular meetings, and giving effective administrative direction. The board exists only when it meets as a board. The board represents citizens because it is impossible for everyone individually to make policy for an organization. Boards can be most helpful in the identification and development of options and recommendations as a first step toward policy development. Board members are also vital in community relations.

The park and recreation professional may work with three

[3] 67 Brokerage Corporation, Wall Street Plaza, New York, NY 10005

different types of boards: policy, coordinating, and advisory. The advisory board is constructed to give advice and counsel. It provides for the expression of ideas and the opinions of groups and has no legal authority for administrative affairs. Policy or administrative boards determine what needs to be done and what parameters are needed to accomplish the desired objectives. The policy board (called a commission in some communities) is usually responsible for needs assessment, appraisal, examining options, developing goals and objectives, and ensuring implementation. The professional staff are called upon often to provide information or background material so policy board members can make informed decisions. The coordinating board usually consists of representatives from several agencies or departments who attempt to analyze what activities are being undertaken. Coordinating boards usually do not have legal authority.

The effective recreation agency board member receives training so that she or he understands the philosophical and conceptual base for recreation and a quality of life, the relationships within the organization, the theoretical and reality base for public service, and methods and procedures for effective operation (Banes, 1975). Board members must realize that they set policy but do not carry it out or become directly involved in administrative duties. Appendix T shows a checklist of what the board member needs to know to be effective. This checklist may be helpful in volunteer board member training as well as in conducting the business of the organization.

Hanlon (1976) suggests several factors that will result in a successful board: broad representation, rotation of members, a committee structure, board manuals listing many of the important details, effective board and staff relationships based on clear job descriptions for each, evaluation mechanisms for the agency, and an orientation system. The individual board member is expected to attend meetings, know his or her duties, heed corporate (public) affairs, file reports, avoid self-dealing, and make no profit from the organization (McCurley, 1978). Being an effective board member is as much a matter of attitude as it is of knowledge. Skills for being an effective board member can be learned, but the enthusiasm and attitude must be developed.

A good board cannot exist without a good staff. If the board makes a bad decision, a number of factors may be responsible. Sometimes staff members do not give all the information. Sometimes the decisions are political. Sometimes decisions are made that do not make sense. However, knowledge is power, and real decision making is often in the hands of information processors instead of decision makers (Bjurburg, 1981). Board members ought to do the best job they can in making decisions based on adequate information, but mistakes can be made.

The recreation, park, and leisure services staff can provide a basis for promoting an effective board. As in other volunteer management situations, the staff member working with the board should make sure the board members have accurate and realistic job descriptions, adequate orientation, regular communication, good working relationships, and opportunities for individual growth. Training is critical for the board member. This includes orientation, on-the-job training, and continuing education opportunities. The board needs to know how to organize itself and develop standing committees. The board members should be helped to create better meetings through such means as catchy meeting announcements, a specific agenda, printed reports, records of the meeting, and simple amenities such as refreshments and a comfortable meeting place. For effective meetings, one must pay attention to where, when, what, who, why, and how (Poummitt, 1983). The use of Roberts Rules of Order may be useful in most situations for all board members to use.

Selection of board members is very important if they are to represent the varied clientele served by park and recreation agencies. Appendix U provides a form for compiling profiles of board members which may be useful in selecting or nominating board members. Representation should be broad based, not one in which the profile of nearly all commission members is the same. The board should be comprised of individuals who have distinct perspectives and strengths, yet who are able to work together effectively. A recent Gallup Poll (1984) showed that 52 percent of the urban residents said they would be willing to serve on an advisory committee, and 64 percent said they would serve on a local committee if asked. This special type of volunteer willing to serve on a board, commission, or committee is available, and the matter of selecting, orienting, and involving them lies at the heart of any successful leisure service venture.

INSURANCE AND RISK MANAGEMENT

Most park, recreation, and leisure service agencies have taken some time to develop risk management plans. These are essential for natural resource and facility areas, but may also be useful for volunteer programs, at least for assessing what potential problems might be. Some of the questions that might be asked include: Is there a risk associated with this volunteer activity? Could the risk be handled in some other way? Does a volunteer have personal coverage or should that be required? Does the staff or agency insurance cover volunteers?

As discussed earlier in this chapter, some people are afraid to volunteer because they are afraid of being sued. Although this rarely happens, it is always a possibility. The degree to which states provide protective legislation for volunteers varies substantially in terms of how the state defines a "qualified" organization, what kinds of volunteer positions are covered, and the scope of protection (Porter, 1988). The solution to the crisis facing America's volunteer community is to exempt all volunteers from civil liability, except for willful and wanton misconduct. States are in various processes of adopting this type of exemption for volunteers. Until that time, however, other measures must be taken.

Insurance programs can offer some protection for volunteers. One should never forget that the best insurance is preventive. In training volunteers, the emphasis should be on thinking before acting. The agency should have insurance, though, to protect both the individual and the organization itself.

According to Aspin and McCurley (1977), there are four kinds of insurance to consider for volunteers: accident, personal liability, auto liability, and board liability. The coverage the agency has for staff may provide a framework for the coverage that should be offered to volunteers. Volunteers should be advised to check their personal, homeowners, and automobile insurance to see what is covered. The agency can cover most of the types of insurance for a volunteer under an umbrella policy. It is important that the agency obtain a clear statement from its insurance carrier concerning the coverage or limitations of insurance for volunteers.

The agency should see if the state worker's compensation program provides coverage for volunteers or if Volunteer Worker's Blanket Accident insurance should be obtained. Volunteer liability insurance covers acts of negligence and can be covered by the organization's comprehensive liability policy. For volunteer professional liability, the person in charge of volunteers should consult the insurance representative. If the position involves driving, volunteers should be asked to carry automobile liability insurance, and it may be necessary to determine if potential volunteers have a suitable driving record before they are selected. The organization may need to carry nonowned and hired car liability insurance in special cases. If volunteers are required to drive for their assignment, the limits of liability should be carefully scrutinized.

Board liability should be obtained for officers and board members. These costs are rising, but the coverage is necessary. It is also possible for the volunteer to use personal liability insurance for the volunteer assignment that is done. Volunteers might get this individually or the organization might provide a way to assist volunteers by obtaining blanket liability insurance.

Specific questions concerning insurance and liability for a particular agency should be addressed directly to the business office, the insurance carrier, or legal counsel. Each situation is slightly different.

TAX DEDUCTIONS

The federal tax laws changed a great deal in the latter half of the 1980s. The leisure service organization should try to get tax information so that volunteers will know what aspects of their volunteer position might be deductible. State income tax laws vary in this regard, but in general all out-of-pocket expenses directly attributable to volunteer services rendered are tax deductible, including food, travel expenses, and tuition for training. Insurance and depreciation are not deductible.

FUND RAISING

Fund raising is a unique way that volunteers can be utilized in an agency. Specific "phonathons" or direct-contact campaigns are often used to solicit money for specific activities. Volunteers who work on these programs are usually short-term volunteers, but they need training similar to that which would be given to anyone working in this capacity.

Not only are fund-raising drives important for raising needed monies, but they can also be used in accomplishing research, in marketing the program, as communication vehicles, and to assist in volunteer recruitment.

In any fund-raising effort, it is good to have one particular focus for the money which is to be collected and specific target audiences to address. Fund raising can be done through direct contact on a person-to-person level, generally from a staff member or active volunteer, or it can be done by a phonathon or direct mail solicitations. In any fund-raising effort, one must keep in mind the costs that will be associated with it: telephone or mailing costs, salaries and incentives, computer costs, printing, and supplies. The leisure service agency might be able to get donations to cover these direct costs of raising money as well. In this day of computers, it is easier to identify and keep contact with potential donors. It is critical to have good lists, to keep track of who has been contacted, and to know what follow-up is needed in terms of additional contacts or thank-you notes.

A fund-raising campaign should be consistent with the agency's overall mission and goals. It is imperative that every contact the agency has with its audience, whether through volunteers or agency staff, reinforces the donor's interest and good feeling about the financial investment she or he is about to make (Galowich & Smith, 1985). Several key questions must be considered in the fund-raising efforts:

1. What is the major reason for the fund-raising effort?

2. Who should be called or contacted?

3. Who should make the contact?

4. How will this effort affect other programs of the leisure service organization?

5. How much money can be raised?

6. When should the effort be undertaken?

7. What is a reasonable cost to raise money in this way?

If volunteers are being used for fund raising, they will need to be heavily involved in the planning as well as the actual efforts. Volunteers can be most useful because they are already familiar with the organization. A planning committee composed of staff and volunteers can be useful in setting goals and addressing the above questions. Volunteers, however, will need training in order to do their jobs most effectively. Opportunities should be provided for volunteers to role play and practice the "art of asking." Possible topics to be included in a training program might be: why people give, how to pepare for the visit or phone contact, conducting the visit/telephone solicitation, fielding questions, and closing the solicitation. Practice sessions which involve role playing followed by a critique are especially useful in building volunteers' fund-raising skills (Goodale, 1987).

A number of good resources exist for conducting effective fund-raising solicitations. It is important to encourage the effective management of volunteers for these events or projects, including appropriate orientation, supervision, and recognition.

CORPORATE VOLUNTEERS

Corporations have been providing funding in a number of ways in recent years. Corporate volunteering refers both to individuals who might volunteer to assist an organization on behalf of the corporation, and to those corporations that provide donations of goods as well as money in the form of sponsorships.

Jasso (1983) has suggested several key steps in attracting the support of corporations. First, the staff member will need to adopt the new roles of detective, business executive, salesperson, and missionary. The detective role involves determining which corporation to contact. This will require some "undercover" work to ascertain who might be a likely donor, who should be contacted, how the contact should be approached, and what information the corporation will need. "Targeting" specific corporations is usually the most successful approach. Second, use contacts to get your foot in the door. Friends, relatives, acquaintances, and agency volunteers can be helpful in finding out who to contact within a corporation. Before making the contact, evaluate the image of the leisure service agency as well as the professional image of the staff. Prepare a presentation about your organization by using a proposal folder that might include a current financial statement, list of the board, statement of purpose, and other pertinent information. Remember, the competition is stiff and resources are limited, so the leisure service provider will want to present the best case possible. Arrange an interview and try to convince the corporation's representative that by satisfying your organization's needs, the person will be satisfying his or her company's needs. Do not take no for an answer until you are absolutely sure the answer is no. Be sure to ask just exactly what needs to be asked to get the person to say yes. Be persistent and patient. Be enthusiastic, but not too enthusiastic. Lastly, once the corporation agrees to help in whatever way, realize that this relationship will need to be nurtured for years to come if it is to continue. All of the above steps will need to be repeated continually.

VOLUNTEERING AS A FEMINIST ISSUE

Volunteers have typically been women in most organizations. Their participation has been very important. In the 1970s, feminist organizations became very critical of the role of women volunteers because of the connotation of "free labor" which was often devalued in that predominant sector of society that focused primarily on monetary rewards. The National Organization for Women (NOW) felt that service-oriented volunteering was detrimental to improving the status of women. Opponents of the criticism of women's volunteering agreed that women needed to have adequate employment opportunities and recognized status, but argued that service-oriented volunteering was not the cause of women's problems.

The result of the dialogue about volunteerism and women has been productive for both the volunteers and the organizations they serve. The organizations began to rethink the ways in which they had always used volunteers. They became more conscious of the need to identify and use each volunteer's interests and abilities, to match appropriate tasks, to provide suitable orientation and training, to involve a broader base of volunteers representative of the community, and to advocate the value of volunteer participation for both women and men (Rubin, 1982). Organizations also began to consciously plan new scheduling and matching techniques to make volunteering more attractive to women. Women also began to consider volunteer activity as a way of developing new educational and employment opportunities. Much of the criticism of women as volunteers abated as these changes occurred, and women volunteers have assumed greater policy-making roles in addition to their direct-service efforts.

A problem concerning volunteerism as a feminist issue will continue to arise as long as society devalues the work of women and as long as value is measured solely in economic terms. On the other hand, the contributions made by women to society through voluntary efforts are becoming more widely acknowledged. In addition, volunteer opportunities have provided a way for women to enrich their lives and to learn skills that can be directly transferred into paying jobs. The conception of volunteers being white, middle-class "do-gooders" has also changed greatly. Today, people of all races, classes, sexes, and ages are volunteering.

Many volunteer agencies have been concerned about the number of women returning to the paid workforce and how this has affected the volunteer ranks. While more women do work today, many women still find the time to volunteer. In addition, with less reliance on the typical young, educated housewife, more people of diverse backgrounds have been recruited into the volunteer ranks. Volunteerism is no longer a feminist issue but two aspects must be kept in mind: the work that women do, whether paid or unpaid, must be valued, and volunteering, whether women or men, is an integral part of what makes our society function as well as it does.

WHY VOLUNTEERS WILL NOT SOLVE ALL THE PROBLEMS

Volunteers are sometimes seen as the panacea for the problems of social service organizations. While they can do much to help, the limitations of using volunteers must also be recognized. This caveat is offered simply to foster a realistic approach to the use of volunteers.

Volunteers are good and helpful, but a recreation, park, and leisure service agency cannot expect that the use of volunteers will solve all its problems. Volunteers can expand, enhance, and extend services, but they cannot do the planning and administration that paid staff are trained to do. Staff should listen to volunteers, but the volunteer role should not administer a program. The major drawback of working with volunteers is that it takes time, money, and energy to work with them. Volunteers do not drop in off the street, ready to teach a class or coach a team. They require recruiting, training, supervision, and recognition, all of which involve personal contact. Unless an agency is willing to make the commitment to providing volunteer management on an ongoing basis, its volunteer program will not be successful.

Volunteers cannot supplant staff. They need direction and guidance from professional staff members. This need for guidance must be paramount when working with volunteers. How many volunteers can a leisure service staff member effectively supervise? This question needs to be considered in planning for enhancing leisure services through volunteers.

BIBLIOGRAPHY

REFERENCES

Acker, P. (1983, March-April). Retention of volunteers. *Minnesota Office of Volunteer Services*, 3–4.

Allen, L., Kraus, R., & Williams-Andy, D. (1986). *Philadelphia Recreation Volunteerism Project.* Philadelphia, PA: City of Philadelphia Department of Recreation and Fairmount Park Commission.

Aspin, M. S., & McCurley, S. (1977, Fall). A guide to insurance for volunteers. *Voluntary Action Leadership*, 16–17.

Ballman, G. (1988, July/August). Addressing concerns across the industry: YMCA: Committed to the community. *Managed Recreation Research Report*, 52–53.

Banes, R. E. (1975, December). Maximizing human resources. *Parks and Recreation*, 27–29, 48.

Bjurburg, R. (1981, October). *Those darn volunteers.* Paper presented at the National Conference on Volunteerism, Philadelphia.

Briggs, D. L. (1982). On satisfying the volunteer and the paid employee: Any difference? *Volunteer Administration, 14*(4), 1–14.

Chambre, S. M. (1982). Recruiting black and Hispanic volunteers: A qualitative study of an organization's experiences. *Journal of Volunteer Administration, 1*(1), 3–10.

Chambre, S. M. (1984). Is volunteering a substitute for role loss in old age? An empirical test of activity theory. *The Gerontologist, 24*(3), 292–298.

DeGrazia, S. (1962). *Of time, work and leisure.* New York: The Twentieth Century Fund.

Ellis, S. J. (Ed.) (1983). *Children as volunteers.* Philadelphia, PA: Energize Associates.

Ellis, S. J. (1985). Daytime volunteers: An endangered species? *Journal of Volunteer Administration, 3*(3), 30–33.

Ellis, S. J. (1986). *From the top down: The executive role in volunteer program success.* Philadelphia, PA: Energize Associates.

Feigley, D. (1988a). *1988 comparative analysis of youth sports educational programs.* New Brunswick, NJ: The Rutgers Youth Sports Research Council.

Feigley, D. (1988b). *State civil immunity legislation: Summaries and interpretations.* New Brunswick, NJ: The Rutgers Youth Sports Research Council.

Gallup, G. (1981, Winter). Americans volunteer 1981 (for independent sector). *Voluntary Action Leadership,* 22–31.

Gallup, G. (1982, Winter). Gallup survey on volunteering. *Voluntary Action Leadership,* 26–29.

Gallup, G. (1984, Winter). The 1983 Gallup survey on volunteering. *Voluntary Action Leadership,* 20–22.

Gallup, G. (1985). *Americans volunteer 1985* (for independent sector). Washington, DC: Author.

Gallup G. (1986, May). Volunteerism in U.S. continues to thrive. *Gallup Reports,* 14–15.

Gallup, G. (1987, Spring). The liability crisis and the use of volunteers by non-profit associations highlighted in advocacy: A Gallup Organization survey conducted for the ASAE Foundation. *Voluntary Action Leadership,* 13–14.

Galowich, R., & Smith, L. (1985, August). The do's and don'ts of telethons—a primer. *Fund Raising Management,* 38, 40, 42, 44, 46, 48.

Gardner, J. (1965). *The anti-leadership vaccine.* New York: The Carnegie Corporation.

Gibson, M. M. (1986). The volunteer's view. *Currents,* 12(4), 64.

Gidron, B. (1983). Sources of job satisfaction among service volunteers. *Journal of Voluntary Action Research,* 12(1), 20–35.

Godbey, G. (1985). *Leisure in your life: An exploration.* State College, PA: Venture Publishing, Inc.

Goodale, T. K. (1987, January). Teaching volunteers the art of asking. *Fund Raising Management,* 32, 35–36, 38.

Goode, E. (1988, November 21). How to bring up children who care. *U.S. News and World Report,* 68–69, 71.

Gray, D. E. (1972, December). Exploring inner space. *Parks and Recreation,* 18–19, 46.

Greer, J. (1985).Volunteers in resource management: A forest service perspective. *The Journal of Volunteer Administration,* 3(4), 1–10.

Haberek, J. (1987, Spring/Summer). Getting H. R. 911 passed: How the process works and what you can do. *Voluntary Action Leadership*, 15–17.

Hanlon, B. (1976). In boards we trust. *Voluntary Action Leadership.*

Harris, L., & Associates. (1975). *The myth and reality of aging in America.* Washington, DC: The National Council on Aging.

Harris, L., & Associates, (1981). *Aging in the eighties: America in transition.* Washington, DC: National Council on Aging, 29–30.

Henderer, J. (1983). Youth volunteers in national parks. *Trends, 20*(4), 21–23.

Henderson, K. (1979). *Motivations and selected characteristics of adult volunteers in extension 4-H youth programs.* Unpublished Ph.D Dissertation, University of Minnesota.

Henderson, K. (1984). Volunteerism as leisure. *Journal of Voluntary Action Research, 13*(1), 55–63.

Hollie, P. G. (1985, September 22). More work, less play. *The New York Times,* Section three, Column 1.

Honer, A. S. (1981). Manage your measurements, don't let them manage you. *Volunteer Administration, 14*(4), 25–29.

Institute for Community Service. (1973). *A process for developing agency based volunteer social work staff.* Appleton, WI: Aid Association for Lutherans.

Jasso, G. (1983). In search of volunteers: How to crack a major corporation. *Journal of Volunteer Administration, 1*(4), 12–16.

Jorgensen, J. D. (1980, July–August). A 14-step planning guide for volunteer trainers. *Minnesota Office of Volunteer Services,* p. 4–5.

Kahn, J. (1985–86, Winter). Legal issues survey results. *The Journal of Volunteer Administration,* 28–34.

Kaplan, M. (1975). *Leisure: Theory and policy.* New York: John Wiley and Sons.

Kennedy, D. S. (1985, Jan–Feb). Staff and volunteer motivation: Helping people overcome discouragement. *The Non-Profit World Report,* 12–13, 30.

Kennedy, D., Austin, D., & Smith, R. (1987). *Special Recreation: Opportunities for persons with disabilities.* Philadelphia, PA: Saunders Publishing, 67–75.

Knowles, M. (1970). *The modern practice of adult education.* New York: Association Press.

MacNeil, R., & Teague, M. (1987). *Aging and leisure: Vitality in later life.* Englewood Cliffs, NJ: Prentice-Hall, 249–252.

Magoon, E. (1978). *Volunteer-staff relationships: A team approach.* Washington State Office of Volunteer Programs. Unpublished manuscript.

Magyar, I. (1983). For the birds: Volunteers in research at the Patuxent Wildlife Research Center. *Trends, 20*(4), 35–38.

Marando, V. L. (1986). Local service delivery: Volunteers and recreation councils. *The Journal of Volunteer Administration, 4*(4), 16–24.

Maslow, A. H. (1943, July). A theory of human motivation. *Psychological Review, 50,* 370–396.

McCurley, S. H. (1978, Sept–Oct). Liabilities and responsibilities of board members of non-profit corporations. *Minnesota Office of Volunteer Services,* 4–5.

McCurley, S. (1987, Spring/Summer). Protecting volunteers from suit: A look at state legislation. *Voluntary Action Leadership,* 17–19.

McGuire, F. & Adams, E. (1986). Older volunteers and outdoor recreation: A nationwide study. *Journal of Park and Recreation Administration, 4*(3), 10–16.

Migliazzo, S. (1983). Are volunteers the answer? *Trends, 20*(3), 17–20.

Minnesota Office of Volunteer Services. (1984). Recruiting alternative sources of volunteers.

Minnesota State Planning Agency. (1979). *Volunteer activities in public outdoor recreation and resources management areas.* St. Paul: Environmental Planning Division.

Moore, N. A. (1978). The application of cost-benefit analysis to volunteer programs. *Volunteer Administration, 11*(1), 13–22.

Moore, R., LaForge, V., & Martorelli, T. (1987). *Organizing outdoor volunteers,* Boston, MA: Appalachian Mountain Club.

Morgan, T. (1986, December 3). Young professionals: New skills in old job of volunteerism. *The New York Times,* C1, C14.

Murphy, J. F. (1975). *Recreation and leisure service.* Dubuque, IA: Wm. C. Brown Co. Publishers.

Nie, N. H., Hull, C. H., Jenkins, J. G., Steinbrenner, K., & Bent,

D. H. (1975). *Statistical Package for the Social Sciences.* New York: McGraw Hill.

O'Brien, M. (1983). Volunteers at New York State historic sites. *Trends, 20*(4), 43–47.

Park, J. M. (1984). The fourth R: The case for releasing volunteers. *Journal of Volunteer Administration, 2*(3), 1–8.

Patton, J. H. (1986–87). Business people volunteer 1986: A survey and analysis. *The Journal of Volunteer Administration, 5*(2), 31–34.

Peat, Marwick, Mitchell & Co. (1987, Spring/Summer). Liability crisis in the making. *Voluntary Action Leadership, 16.*

Popowski, K. J. (1985). Youth views on volunteering and service learning from the Chicago area youth poll. *The Journal of Volunteer Administration, 3*(4), 34–41.

Porter, J. E. (1988). Volunteers: The fight for survival. *Leadership, 12–13,* 15, 50.

Poummitt, M. R. (1983, Sept–Oct). Are your board meetings bored meetings? *Nonprofit World Report, 16–18,* 35.

President's Commission on Americans Outdoors: Case studies. (1986a, December). Washington, DC: U.S. Government Printing Office.

President's Commission on Americans Outdoors: Report and recommendations to the President. (1986b, December) Washington, DC: U.S. Government Printing Office.

Price, B. (1984, February 27). Looking for a few good volunteer park rangers. *The Philadelphia Inquirer.*

Proudfoot, M. B. (1978). Communication skills. *Volunteer Administration, 11*(1), 32–37.

Pryor, J. (1982). A volunteer program evaluation checklist. *Minnesota Office of Volunteer Services,* 5–6.

Rawls, C. (1983). National volunteer project. *Trends, 20*(4), 8–11.

Republican National Committee (1984). *Community partnership manual: Working together at the local level.* Washington, DC: Author.

Rippel, P. W. (1978). *Planning organizational goals and roles.* Unpublished manuscript.

Robins, H. P. (1982). Eyeball to eyeball. *Case Currents, 8*(9), 20–22.

Rubin, S. G. (1982). The dialogue between voluntarism and feminism: Implications for higher education. In E. Greenberg (Ed.), *New directions for experiential education*. San Francisco: Jossey-Bass.

Scheier, I. (1978, Summer). Time to reconsider. *Voluntary Action Leadership*, 38–39.

Scheier, I. (1980). *Exploring volunteer space: The recruiting of a nation*. Boulder, Co: Volunteer Readership.

Schindler, A., & Chastain, D. (1980, Sept–Oct). Careful planning and effective management—qualities of a successful trainer. *Minnesota Office of Volunteer Services*, 5–6.

Schindler-Rainman, E., & Lippitt, R. (1971). *The volunteer community*. Washington, DC: Center for a Voluntary Society.

Schwartz, J. C. (1982, Jan–Feb). Training volunteers. *Minnesota Office of Volunteer Services*, 6.

Selvidge, N. (1978). Marketing Volunteers. *Volunteer Administration*, *10*(4), 12–15.

Shank, J. (1984, February). Employing disabled persons in leisure service agencies. *Parks and Recreation*, 50–54, 70.

Tedrick, T. (1975). *The influence of the Foster Grandparent and Retired Senior Volunteer Programs as perceived by older participants*. Unpublished master's thesis, Pennsylvania State University.

Tedrick, T., & Wagoner, H. S. (1985, Fall). The New York State Volunteer Coaches Institute: A key to the survival of local youth sports. *The Voice*, 28–31.

Trudeau, R. (1983). Volunteer programs in the East Bay Regional Park District. *Trends*, *20*(4), 39–42.

United Media Enterprises. (1983). *Where does the time go?* New York: Newspaper Enterprise Association, 45–49.

Utterback, J. & Heyman, S. R. (1984). An examination of methods in the evaluation of volunteer programs. *Evaluation and Program Planning*, 7, 229–235.

Vineyard, S. (1984). Recruiting and retaining volunteers: No gimmicks, no gags. *Journal of Volunteer Administration*, *2*(3), 23–28.

Volunteers In Parks. (1982). (Brochure outlining legislation and intent.) Harrisburg, PA: Bureau of State Parks.

Watts, A. D., & Edwards, P. K. (1983). Recruiting and retaining human service volunteers: An empirical analysis. *Journal of Voluntary Action Research*, *12*(3), 9–22.

Wilson, M. (1976). *The effective management of volunteer programs.* Boulder, CO: Volunteer Management Associates.
Wilson, M. (1984, July). The new frontier: Volunteer management training. *Training and Development Journal,* 50–55.

ADDITIONAL READINGS

Allen, K. (1982, Sept–Oct). Kenn Allen addresses VFM Conference. *Minnesota Office of Volunteer Services,* 3–6.
Allen, K., McCurley, S., & Mosel, D. (1982). *Will volunteering survive?* Washington, DC: The National Center of Citizen Involvement.
Corporate Volunteer Coordinator's Council. (1984). The virtues of volunteering. *Personnel Journal, 63*(8), 42–44, 45–48.
Dorang, E. S. (1981, March). A UNA-Organized hospice volunteer program. *Nursing Outlook,* 170–173.
Eggert, J. D. (1984). Program evaluation. In V. Lawson (Ed.), *Management handbook for volunteer programs.* Syracuse, NY: Literacy Volunteers of America, Inc.
Gallup, G. (1981). Volunteers: America's best hope for the future. *Minnesota Office of Volunteer Services,* 3–5.
Hanlon, B. (1975, Summer). Is anybody listening? *Voluntary Action Leadership.*
Hardy, P. (1981). Experiences and training records: Volunteer recognition that counts. *Volunteer Administration, 11*(1), 27–29.
Hardy, R. (1982). Guidelines for the physical education major. *Journal of Physical Education, Recreation, and Dance, 53*(3), 72–73.
Highet, G. (1950). *The art of teaching.* New York: Knopf.
Ilsley, P. J., & Niemi, J. A. (1981). *Recruiting and training volunteers.* New York: McGraw-Hill.
Implications for Volunteers in Extension. (1984). *National Projections.* Madison, WI: University of Wisconsin, Department of Continuing and Vocational Education.
Junior League of St. Paul, Inc. (1977). *A handbook for administrators of volunteers.* St. Paul: Voluntary Action Council.

Kreisel, M. J. (n.d.) *Motivations and social characteristics of active volunteers in three Alberta trial organizations.* Alberta, Canada: University of Alberta, Department of Recreation and Leisure Studies.

Lynch, R. (1982, Jan–Feb), Training volunteers, *Minnesota Office of Volunteer Services,* 3–5.

McCurley, S. H. (1980, May–June). How much are volunteers worth? *Minnesota Office of Volunteer Services,* 4–5.

McDuff, N. L. (1987, Spring). Volunteer recruiting teams. *Journal of Volunteer Administration,* 4–6.

Minnesota Office of Volunteer Services. (1984). Insurance coverage for volunteers.

Minnesota Office of Volunteer Services. (1984). The unemployed person in the volunteer workforce.

Moore, W. M. (1987). Volunteers: A changing scene. *Fund Raising Management, 17*(11), 56, 58.

Mosel, D. (1982, Nov–Dec). How to plan for a productive and satisfactory meeting. *Minnesota Office of Volunteer Services,* 3–5.

Moyer, K. L. (1982, January). Four steps to effective community involvement. *Educational Leadership,* 285–287.

National Councils of YMCAs. (1978). *Voluntarism: Confrontation and opportunity.* New York: National Council of YMCAs.

Navaratnam, K. K. (1986, Fall). Volunteer training volunteers: A model for human service organizations. *Journal of Volunteer Administration,* 19–25.

Neddermeyer, D. M. (1983, Sept–Oct). Volunteering in America: Are you getting your fair share? *Non-profit World Report,* 19–21.

Park, J. M. (1983) *Meaning well is not enough.* South Plainfield, NJ: Groupwork Today, Inc.

Pocock, J. W. (1981). Fly right with volunteers. *Case Currents,* 20–23.

Pokrass, R. J. (1986). Fire when ready. *Currents, 12*(4), 20–23.

Ray, G. W. (1982). Meeting volunteers on their own ground. In E. Greenberg (Ed.), *New directions in experiential learning.* San Francisco: Jossey-Bass.

Scheier, I. (1978). *Winning with staff: A new look at staff support for volunteers.* Boulder, CO: Volunteer Readership.

Schindler-Rainman, E. (1982). Trends and changes in the volunteer world. *Journal of Voluntary Action Research, 11*(2–3), 157–163.

Tedrick, R., Davis, W. & Coutant, G. (1984). Effective management of a volunteer corp. *Parks and Recreation, 19*(2), 55–60.

Appendices

Appendix A Survey questionnaire: The use of
volunteers within leisure service agencies

Please take a few moments to complete this questionnaire. Most items
require only a check in the appropriate column; a few require a brief
written response.

Section I. Background Information

1. How many full-time staff are there within your leisure service
   agency or department?

   Fewer than five   _____
   6–10   _____
   11–24   _____
   25–50   _____
   More than 50   _____

2. If you work for a local government agency, what is the size of the
   population within your borders?

   Fewer than 20,000   _____
   21,000–50,000   _____
   51,000–100,000   _____
   101,000–250,000   _____
   Over 250,000   _____
   Not Applicable   _____

3. Which description most clearly resembles your leisure service
   agency or department?

   A private, for-profit organization   _____
   A publicly supported, local
      government department   _____
   A publicly supported, state
      government department   _____
   A quasi-public agency supported
      through local funds and
      donations from organizations
      such as the United Way   _____
   Other   _____
      Briefly describe:

123

4. Is the primary thrust of your organization or agency therapeutic recreation services?

     Yes   _____

     No   _____

Section II. Characteristics of the Volunteer Program

1. Our agency has one person assigned the role of coordinating volunteers.

     Yes   _____

     No   _____

     Not Sure   _____

2. Our agency spends an adequate amount of time in planning our volunteer program.

     Yes   _____

     No   _____

     Not Sure   _____

3. Our agency has written job descriptions for volunteers.

     Yes   _____

     No   _____

     Not Sure   _____

4. All volunteers sign a written contract.

     Yes   _____

     No   _____

     Not Sure   _____

5. Our agency has clear policies on recruiting, assigning, and evaluating volunteers.

     Yes   _____

     No   _____

     Not Sure   _____

6. Inservice training is provided our volunteers on a regular basis.

     Yes   _____

     No   _____

     Not Sure   _____

7. Our agency regularly evaluates volunteers and meetings are held to review progress.

     Yes   _____

     No   _____

     Not Sure   _____

8. Formal records are kept on all volunteers.

      Yes   _____
      No   _____
      Not Sure   _____

9. Our agency has a procedure manual which all volunteers are given.

      Yes   _____
      No   _____
      Not Sure   _____

10. Our agency keeps annual records on the amount of hours volunteered and the dollar amount that time represents.

      Yes   _____
      No   _____
      Not Sure   _____

11. Experienced volunteers are able to assume more responsibility within our organization.

      Yes   _____
      No   _____
      Not Sure   _____

12. Our paid staff are recognized for their contribution to the volunteer program.

      Yes   _____
      No   _____
      Not Sure   _____

Section III. Evaluation of the Volunteer Program

1. Currently our agency has an effective volunteer program.

Strongly   Strongly
Agree ____ Agree ____ Disagree ____ Disagree ____ Not Sure ____

2. The goals of our volunteer program are written and understood by those in our agency.

Strongly   Strongly
Agree ____ Agree ____ Disagree ____ Disagree ____ Not Sure ____

3. Our clients or program participants are receptive to volunteer staff.

Strongly   Strongly
Agree ____ Agree ____ Disagree ____ Disagree ____ Not Sure ____

4. Our agency does a good job in recruiting volunteers.

Strongly   Strongly
Agree _____   Agree _____   Disagree _____   Disagree _____   Not Sure _____

5. On the whole our staff is very supportive of volunteers.

Strongly   Strongly
Agree _____   Agree _____   Disagree _____   Disagree _____   Not Sure _____

6. Our volunteers receive regular feedback on how they are doing.

Strongly   Strongly
Agree _____   Agree _____   Disagree _____   Disagree _____   Not Sure _____

7. Our agency offers excellent recognition of volunteers.

Strongly   Strongly
Agree _____   Agree _____   Disagree _____   Disagree _____   Not Sure _____

8. Our agency's volunteer program is considered another "leisure" opportunity for people.

Strongly   Strongly
Agree _____   Agree _____   Disagree _____   Disagree _____   Not Sure _____

9. Our agency finds it relatively easy to motivate volunteers.

Strongly   Strongly
Agree _____   Agree _____   Disagree _____   Disagree _____   Not Sure _____

10. We are able to retain the same volunteers from year to year.

Strongly   Strongly
Agree _____   Agree _____   Disagree _____   Disagree _____   Not Sure _____

Section IV. The Present and Future Uses of Volunteers

List the 3 programs or areas in which your volunteers are *most* successful.

      1. _____
      2. _____
      3. _____

List the 3 programs or areas that could most benefit through better use of volunteers.

      1. _____
      2. _____
      3. _____

Looking to the future, list 3 new roles that you would like to see volunteers occupy in your agency.

1. _____
2. _____
3. _____

Appendix B–1   Characteristics of the volunteer program

Characteristic	Yes	No	Not sure
One person assigned as volunteer coordinator	43.8	53.78	2.5
Adequate time for planning the volunteer program	38.7	51.3	10.0
Written job descriptions for volunteers	50.0	46.2	3.7
Volunteers sign a written contract	28.8	66.2	5.0
Clear policies on recruiting, assigning, evaluating volunteers	28.8	61.2	10.0
Inservice training provided on a regular basis	48.7	46.2	5.0
Volunteers regularly evaluated and meetings held to review progress	27.5	65.0	7.5
Formal records kept on volunteers	43.8	48.7	7.5
Volunteers given a procedural manual	30.0	66.2	3.7
Annual record kept on amount of hours volunteered and dollar amount represented	42.5	46.2	11.2
Experienced volunteers assume more responsibility	80.0	15.0	5.0
Paid staff recognized in assisting volunteer program	36.2	53.7	10.0

Percentages

Appendix B–2   Evaluation of the volunteer program

Characteristics	Percentages				
	Strongly agree	Agree	Disagree	Strongly disagree	Not sure
Agency has an effective volunteer program	10.0	38.7	33.7	13.7	3.7
Goals of volunteer program are written and understood	6.3	28.8	36.2	16.2	12.5
Clients/participants receptive to volunteers	31.3	55.0	3.7	3.7	6.3
Good job in recruiting volunteers	13.7	40.0	23.8	18.8	3.7
Staff very supportive of volunteers	28.8	61.2	5.0	1.2	3.7
Volunteers receive feedback on how they are doing	7.5	43.8	32.5	7.5	8.8
Excellent recognition of volunteers by agency	11.2	47.5	25.0	10.0	6.3
Volunteer program is considered a "leisure" opportunity	7.5	41.3	25.0	6.3	20.0
Easy to motivate volunteers	5.0	48.7	26.2	7.5	12.5
Some volunteers retained from year to year	7.5	65.0	11.2	6.3	10.0

Appendix C–1   Chi-square analysis of survey: Number of full-time staff by whether the volunteer is evaluated and meetings held to review progress

Staff size	Response Yes	No
Fewer than 5	6 (27.3%)	28 (53.8%)
6–10	5 (25.0%)	12 (75.0%)
11–24	5 (50.0%)	5 (50.0%)
25–50	4 (100.0%)	0 (0.0%)
More than 50	3 (30.0%)	7 (70.0%)

Chi-square = 13.97 with 4 d.f.; significance .007
Crammer's V = .43

Appendix C–2   Chi-square analysis of survey: Size of population served by whether a volunteer coordinator is present

Size of Population served	Response Yes	No
Fewer than 50,000	4 (21.1%)	15 (78.9%)
51,000–250,000	3 (30.0%)	7 (70.0%)
More than 250,000	8 (66.7%)	4 (33.3%)

Chi-square = 6.84 with 2 d.f.; significance .03
Crammer's V = .41

Appendix C–3   Chi-square analysis: Therapeutic or non-therapeutic thrust by whether a volunteer coordinator is present

Primary Thrust	Response Yes	No
Therapeutic Recreation	12 (75.0%)	4 (25.0%)
Non-Therapeutic Recreation	23 (37.1%)	39 (62.9%)

Chi-square = 5.93 with 1 d.f.; significance .01
phi = .31

Appendix C–4   Chi-square analysis: Therapeutic or non-therapeutic thrust by whether the agency does a good job recruiting volunteers

| | Response | |
Primary Thrust	Yes	No
Therapeutic Recreation	4 (28.6%)	10 (71.4%)
Non-Therapeutic Recreation	39 (61.9%)	24 (38.1%)

Chi-square = 3.90 with 1 d.f.; significance .05
phi = .26

Appendix D–1   Code of responsibility for volunteers

BE SURE	Look into your heart and know that you really want to help other people.
BE CONVINCED	Do not offer your services unless you believe in the value of what you are doing.
BE LOYAL	Offer suggestions, but don't "knock."
ACCEPT THE RULES	Don't criticize what you don't understand. There may be a good reason.
SPEAK UP	Ask about things you don't understand. Don't coddle your doubts and frustrations until they drive you away, or turn you into a problem worker.
BE WILLING TO LEARN	Training is essential to any job well done.
KEEP ON LEARNING	Know all you can about your agency and your job.
WELCOME SUPERVISION	You will do a better job and enjoy it more if you are doing what is expected of you.
BE DEPENDABLE	Your word is your bond. Do what you have agreed to do. Don't make promises you can't keep.
BE A TEAM PLAYER	Find a place for yourself ON THE TEAM. The lone operator is pretty much out of place in today's complex community.

Source: Joey Bishop, Coordinator of Volunteer Services, Des Moines, Iowa

Appendix D–2   Bill of rights for volunteers

THE RIGHT TO BE TREATED AS A CO-WORKER . . . not just free help . . . not as a prima donna.

THE RIGHT TO A SUITABLE ASSIGNMENT . . . with consideration for personal preference, temperament, life experience, education and employment background.

THE RIGHT TO KNOW AS MUCH ABOUT THE AGENCY AS POSSIBLE . . . its policies . . . its people . . . its programs.

THE RIGHT TO TRAINING FOR THE JOB . . . thoughtfully planned and effectively presented training.

THE RIGHT TO CONTINUING EDUCATION ON THE JOB . . . as a follow-up to initial training . . . information about new developments—training for greater responsibility.

THE RIGHT TO SOUND GUIDANCE AND DIRECTION . . . by someone who is experienced, patient, well-informed and thoughtful . . . and who has the time to invest in giving guidance.

THE RIGHT TO A PLACE TO WORK . . . an orderly, designated place . . . conducive to work . . . and worthy of the job to be done.

THE RIGHT TO PROMOTION AND A VARIETY OF EXPERIENCES . . . through advancement to assignments of more responsibility . . . through transfer from one activity to another . . . through special assignment.

THE RIGHT TO BE HEARD . . . to have a part in planning . . . to feel free to make suggestions . . . to have respect shown for an honest opinion.

THE RIGHT TO RECOGNITION . . . in the form of promotion . . . awards . . . through day-by-day expressions of appreciation . . . and by being treated as a bona fide co-worker.

Source: Joey Bishop, Coordinator of Volunteer Services, Des Moines, Iowa

Appendix E Volunteer position planning worksheet

Tasks To Be Done	# of Volunteers Needed	Frequency of Participation	Job Importance	Expertise Needed

Appendix F–1   Worksheet: Volunteer position description

Agency: _____ Service Unit: _____

Position: _____

1. Purpose of the job:

2. Responsibilities and Duties:

3. Supervisory Plan:

Qualifications:

Time Required:

Commitment Required:

Comments:

Appendix F–2 Volunteer position description: Special events helper

Special events helpers will assist in the planning and/or implementation of social activities scheduled periodically for MSers. The purpose of the special events program is to provide the opportunity for social activities and experiences for MS patients. All special events helpers will be required to take the two-day general communications training session. When necessary, additional information and instruction will be given by staff immediately prior to the event.

At an interview with the Volunteer Coordinator, the Special Events Helper will choose one or more of the following activities in which to participate:

1. *Cultural events.* Volunteers are needed in two areas. Some volunteers will serve on a steering committee and work with staff to organize events. Responsibilities of this committee will be to organize one event a month, publicize it in the MS newsletter, arrange for tickets to be ordered, and help to arrange transportation. Volunteers who work at the event will help the MSers attending with their coats, escort them to their seats, and help them onto the bus.

2. *Christmas party.* The volunteers will assist MSers as they arrive, help with coats, serve refreshments, and assist in any other ways needed to make the party an enjoyable one for the guests.

3. *Twins baseball games.* Approximately four games a year are scheduled. Volunteers will attend the games with the MSers, assist with seating, obtain and serve refreshments, and, in general, share the experience with the MSers. A commitment to all four games would be ideal. However, if this is not possible for the volunteer, any number the volunteers can commit to would be acceptable.

4. *Picnic.* The volunteers will pick up the food, organize the food, grill, plates, drinks, etc., before the picnic begins. During the picnic, volunteers will help serve food and make the event an enjoyable social experience for the MSers.

Following the event, the Volunteer Coordinator will contact the special events helpers so they can evaluate the experience together and discuss the possibility of plans for future volunteer involvement in other special events.

Example from:

MINNESOTA NORTH STAR CHAPTER
NATIONAL MULTIPLE SCLEROSIS SOCIETY
4306 West 36½ Street
Minneapolis, MN 55416

Appendix G Community groups that can help

Type of organization	Name	Contact person & telephone #	Purpose of organization	Meeting information	Other
Religious					
Political					
Fraternal					
Service					
Corporations					
Civic					
Social					
Professional					
Educational					
Military					
Self-Help					
Hobby Clubs					
Unions					
Business					

Appendix H   Sample illustration of recruitment brochure

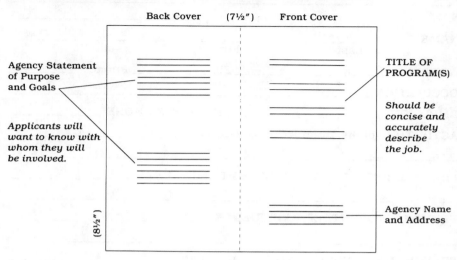

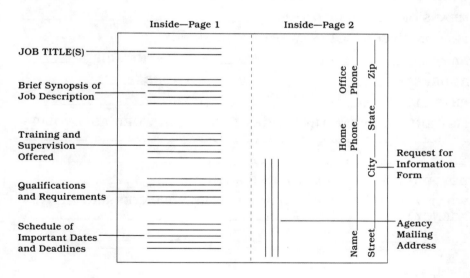

Appendix I Volunteer application

Date_____

NAME_____
             Last   First   Middle

ADDRESS_____ Zip_____ Phone_____

OCCUPATION_____

EMPLOYER_____ BUSINESS PHONE_____

ACTIVITIES (clubs, organizations, church groups)_____
_____

LIST HOBBIES, SPECIAL SKILLS AND INTERESTS_____
_____

PREVIOUS VOLUNTEER EXPERIENCE_____
_____

WHAT HOURS/DAYS ARE YOU AVAILABLE?_____

MEANS OF TRANSPORTATION_____

PERSON TO CONTACT IN CASE OF EMERGENCY:

NAME_____ RELATIONSHIP_____

ADDRESS_____ PHONE_____

PHYSICIAN_____ PHONE_____

LIST ANY HANDICAP THAT MIGHT LIMIT YOUR WORK AS A VOLUN-
TEER_____
_____

HOW DID YOU HEAR ABOUT THIS AGENCY?_____

WHAT WOULD YOU LIKE TO ACHIEVE BY VOLUNTEERING AT THIS
AGENCY?_____
_____
_____

Appendix J Placing volunteers

◯ = Volunteer's Skills

☐ = Volunteer Position

Volunteer's skills are not being adequately used.

Position is too much for the volunteer. She/he is likely to become frustrated.

Volunteer will be able to perform the job adequately but will need additional challenges.

Best situation. Volunteer will be challenged to expand within the job.

Appendix K Volunteer agreement form

AGREEMENT BETWEEN_____(AGENCY)

_____(VOLUNTEER)

on the terms of volunteer service

The_____(Agency) agrees to:

1. Provide all necessary orientation, training and supervision for the volunteer position.

2. Provide continuing education, conferences and workshops for volunteers, to enable them to exchange ideas, suggestions and recommendations.

3. Change the volunteer assignment or add new duties only through mutual agreement between the volunteer and his/her supervisor.

4. Conduct a periodic evaluation of the volunteer's performance, keep records of length of service, maintain a personnel file and provide the volunteer with a letter of reference when requested.

5. Offer volunteer opportunities for more responsible volunteer jobs with the agency's program when appropriate and available.

6. (Optional) The_____(Agency) agrees to provide_____benefits. (Example: uniforms, free parking, lunches, etc.)

The volunteer_____agrees to:

1. Become familiar with and adhere to the policies and procedures of the agency.

2. Attend orientation sessions, on-the-job training and continuing education programs when possible.

3. _____(volunteer) agrees to perform _____(hours, days of service) at _____ (Agency) in the position of_____ (job).

4. Provide at least 24 hours notice to the agency if he/she will be unable to work. (Except in case of sudden illness or emergency).

5. Give prior notice if volunteer work is to be terminated or interrupted for an extended period of time.

6. Facilitate recordkeeping by signing in and out when working and wearing identification when required.

7. Protect confidential information and exercise good judgment when acting on the agency's behalf.

8. Maintain a nonjudgmental attitude with clients.

9. Accept supervision with a willingness to learn and a willingness to ask about things you don't understand.

Volunteer	Agency	Date

Appendix L Training setting checklist

Physical surroundings	Human and interpersonal relations	Organizational
Space	Welcoming	Policy
Lighting	Comfortable Setting	Structure
Acoustics/Outside Noise	Informality	Clientele
Decor	Warm-up Exercises	Meeting Announcements
Temperature/Ventilation	Democratic Leadership	Informational Literature
Seating Arrangement and Comfort	Interpersonal Relations	Program Theme
Refreshments	Handling VIPs	Advertising
Writing Materials	Mutual Planning	Posters/Displays
Ashtrays/Coat Racks	Assessing Needs	Exhibits
Rest Rooms	Formulating Objectives	Budget and Finance
	Designing and Implementing Activities	Publish Agenda and Closing Time
Audiovisual Aids		Frequency of Scheduled Meetings
Parking and Directions	Evaluation	
Name Tags or Cards	Closing Exercise	
	Close on Time	

Appendix M   Meeting effectiveness checklist

	Yes	No
1. Are meetings held during convenient hours?	___	___
2. Do you have a planned agenda?	___	___
3. Do volunteers or committee members have a part in the planning?	___	___
4. Are meetings generally too long in length?	___	___
5. Are meetings dominated by a few?	___	___
6. Does the administrator dominate the meeting?	___	___
7. Are materials handed out and then read word for word?	___	___
8. Is adequate time allowed for discussion of mutual problems?	___	___
9. Do meetings move too slowly?	___	___
10. Are agendas handed out before the meeting?	___	___
11. Is "hedge hopping" (beating around the bush) present?	___	___
12. Are decisions reached based upon previous prejudices?	___	___
13. Do volunteers (committee members) understand the purpose of the meeting?	___	___
14. Are individuals criticized before the entire group?	___	___
15. Do your meetings wander aimlessly off the topic?	___	___
16. Are the physical surroundings adequate?	___	___
17. Are meetings interrupted frequently by outside circumstances?	___	___
18. Do you start and finish meetings on time?	___	___
19. Could the agenda be taken care of just as well by a memorandum?	___	___
20. Do volunteers (committee members) keep coming back to future meetings?	___	___

Appendix N   Sample recordkeeping for volunteers

5×8 card

Side one:

> Name _____ Phone _____
>
> Address _____
>
> Contact In Case of Emergency _____
>
> Volunteer Record: (Put dates and times and any other notes)
>
>
>
>
> _____
>
> Side two
>
> _____
>
> Training Received: (Type, duration, instructor, date, resources provided)
>
>
>
> Recognition Given: (date, what, where, by whom)
>
>
>
> Comments:

Appendix O Test your performance with volunteers

1. Do you always think out exactly what you want a volunteer to do? (a) Always (b) Sometimes

2. When a volunteer writes or telephones offering help, do you (a) reply at once? (b) reply after a few days? (c) reply after two weeks? or because you are not in need of volunteers (d) make no reply?

3. Do you clearly inform your volunteers about: (a) your organization—its aims and achievements? (b) office hours? (c) when best to reach you by telephone? (d) who's who in your agency?

4. Do all your volunteers know how to claim their expenses? (a) Yes (b) No

5. Do you encourage volunteers to meet with you (a) at regular intervals? (b) when they need help?

6. Do you give volunteers adequate guidelines on when to seek your advice and help? (a) Yes (b) No

7. 1. Do you listen to volunteers' comments? (a) Yes (b) No
   2. Do you encourage volunteers to express their views? (a) Yes (b) No
   3. Do you take up their suggestions for giving better service, or where this is not possible, explain why? (a) Yes (b) No

8. Do you always remember to thank your volunteers? (a) after a particularly good job has been done? (b) on leaving? (c) on offering their services?

9. Do you know your volunteers' addresses and telephone numbers and do you have a written record of these? (a) Yes (b) No

10. Do you try to find out why volunteers leave when no reason is given? (a) Yes (b) No

11. Do you provide (a) some preparation for the job? (b) some continuous training? (c) suggestions for visits of observation, books to read?

12. Do you (a) provide opportunities for suitable volunteers to progress to more responsible jobs? (b) discover their special skills then make the best use of them?

13. Do you help volunteers to feel part of your organization by: (a) including them in staff meetings where appropriate? (b) having a vol-

unteer bulletin board/newsletter? (c) insisting on good work standards? (d) informing them of plans and progress?

14. Do you use (a) written job descriptions? (b) written contracts?

15. Do you use a volunteer procedures manual for (a) planning? (b) training? (c) supervising? (d) evaluating?

16. Is your entire staff supportive of volunteers? (a) Always (b) Sometimes

Adapted from Joey Bishop, Coordinator of Volunteer Services, Des Moines, Iowa

Appendix P–1 Sample (to be adapted to agency requirements)

VOLUNTEER SELF-EVALUATION FORM

PROGRAM _____

Confidential

1. As a volunteer, did you enjoy your assignment? Yes No
   Generally

2. About how long did your assignment last? _____

3. Did the program demand a reasonable or unreasonable amount of your time? _____

4. About how much time per week did you spend? _____

5. Did you have good communication with:

Staff	Yes	Generally	No
Unit Supervisor	Yes	Generally	No
Coordinator	Yes	Generally	No
Client	Yes	Generally	No

6. If you needed assistance, was it given promptly?
   Yes Generally No Anything specific? _____

7. Do you think the program was too rigid? Yes Generally No
   too loose? Yes Generally No
   Please explain: _____

8. Did you receive benefit from the monthly meetings? _____
   Any suggestions? _____
   _____

9. What was of most value to you? _____
   _____

10. Do you wish to be reassigned? _____
    PROGRAM _____ WHEN? _____

11. Do you have any friends you would recommend as volunteers?
    _____
    If so, please list:

    Signature _____
    Date _____

Appendix P–2 Profile of volunteer-staff characteristics*

Instructions:

1. Please mark each item below with an "n" at the point on the scale which in your experience best describes your organization now.

2. Then mark each item with a check (X) where you would like to have it be with regard to that item.

Note: Please check if you are: Paid Staff _____   Volunteer _____

I. *LEADERSHIP:*

	System 1 Virtually none	System 2 Some	System 3 Substantial amount	System 4 A great deal
1. How much confidence and trust does staff have in volunteers?	Virtually none	Some	Substantial amount	A great deal
2. How much confidence and trust do volunteers have in staff?	Not very free	Somewhat free	Quite free	Very free
3. How free do you feel to talk to your immediate volunteer or staff supervisor about your job?	Seldom	Sometimes	Often	Very frequently
4. How often are your ideas sought and used constructively by your volunteer or staff supervisor?	Discouraged Almost never occurs	Occasionally occurs	Encouraged most levels	Good at all levels
5. How do you feel about delegation of authority?				

II. *MOTIVATION:*

	Minimal recognition, personal involvement, and achievement	Moderate recognition, involvement and achievement	Frequent recognition, some involvement, marginal achievement	Optimum involvement, personal enrichment and achievement
1. The motivational forces used most in organization are:				
2. Who feels responsibility for achieving the goals of this organization?	Top administration	Top administration and Board volunteers	Most people who work here	Everyone—admin., staff and volunteers
3. How much cooperative teamwork exists				
a. between members of paid staff?	Very little	Relatively little	Moderate amount	Great deal
b. between volunteers and paid staff?				
c. between volunteers?				
4. How much satisfaction do you derive from your job and your achievements here?	Very little	Moderate amount	Adequate	Very high

III. *COMMUNICATION:*

Question	Very little	Some	Quite a bit	Much, with both individuals & groups
1. What is the amount of interaction and communication aimed at achieving the goals?	Very little	Some	Quite a bit	Much, with both individuals & groups
2. What is the usual direction of the flow of information?	Downward	Mostly downward	Down & up	Down, up, and sideways
3. How well do supervisors comprehend problems faced by their volunteers and professional staff?	Not very well	Rather well	Quite well	Very well
4. How would you rate the general communications between staff & volunteers?	Poor	Need more	Adequate	Very good

IV. DECISIONS:

1. At what levels are decisions made?

Mostly at top levels	Policy decisions made at top, some delegation	Broad policy at top, more delegation	Decision making done throughout organization

2. Are volunteers involved in decision making process?

Very seldom	Superficially but not in serious matters	Adequate involvement	Their involvement is sought at all decision making levels

3. Are volunteers and professional staff involved in decisions relating to their work?

   a. Paid Staff

   b. Volunteers

Almost never	Occasionally consulted	Generally consulted	Fully involved

V. GOALS:

	By management and staff to volunteers in condescending manner	By Board volunteers to staff in an arbitrary manner	By select management, staff and volunteers in a controlling manner	By management, staff & volunteers in a democratic manner
1. How are agency goals established?				
2. Do you have the opportunity to set goals for your job?	Never	Seldom	Occasionally	Usually
3. How well informed are most members of this organization of the goals?	Know very little	Vague knowledge	Adequately informed	Well informed
4. Are your personal goals being met in your present job?	Not at all	Minimally	Adequately	Very well

VI. GENERAL KNOWLEDGE:

	Inhibits initiative and achievement	Sometimes conducive but with many restrictions	Adequately conducive	Extremely conducive
1. *Physical Facilities.* Extent to which the physical facilities and equipment within the office are conducive to creative initiative and achievement.				
2. Extent to which printed internal communications serve as information tool.	Inadequate information flow	Information flow adequate	Information flows very well	Keeps everyone well informed
3. Extent of my personal knowledge and understanding of:	Almost none	Limited	Adequate	Excellent
A. the programs of this agency				
B. mission and principles of this agency				
C. the policies				
4. *Image.* Within your personal contacts what response do you get regarding the image of the agency in the community?	Negative	Disinterested	Vague	Positive

*Adapted by Marlene Wilson from an instrument used in industry (Rensis Likert).

Appendix P–3 Volunteer personnel evaluation

Volunteer _____

Home Address: _____

Volunteer Period: from _____ to _____

Position Held: _____ Tel: _____

Rated by: _____

_____ (title)

Date: _____

	Excellent	Good	Fair	Poor	Not Observed

1. PERSONALITY AND ATTITUDE:

   A. Cheerful and friendly with everyone

   B. Alert for new ideas

   C. Cooperative attitude toward fellow volunteers, supervisors and other participants

   D. Suitable personality for position

   E. Interest in and loyalty to the agency and discretion in discussing it and its policies

2. POSITION DESCRIPTION (list specific responsibilities and rate)

   A.

   B.

   C.

   D.

E.

COMMENTS: _____

3. LEADERSHIP:

   A. An example to others

   B. Not content with the status quo; constantly trying to improve both program and himself

   C. Has an ability to provide leadership

   D. Enthusiastic

   E. Skills and past experience enrich program

4. RELIABILITY:

   A. Is punctual in meeting all time schedules

   B. Accepts full share of responsibility

   C. Carries out, in cooperative spirit, policies and requirements

   COMMENTS: _____

5. OTHER (All other concerns): _____

   REMARKS & FUTURE: _____

Appendix P–4 State of New York—Department of Correctional Services, Correctional Volunteer Services Program

VOLUNTEER SERVICES PROGRAM EVALUATION

FOR VOLUNTEER SERVICES PROGRAM USE ONLY

FACILITY/AREA OFFICE:

PROGRAM:

PROVIDED BY:

To provide the best possible volunteer services, we are constantly examining our activities and attempting to improve the programs provided inmates and parolees. To reach this goal, I need your assistance. Please answer the questions on this form and return it in the addressed envelope provided. All replies will be treated in confidence. Signing your reply is optional.

Thank you for your assistance.

COORDINATOR, VOLUNTEER SERVICES PROGRAM

1. You are a:
   Correction Officer ☐
   Inmate ☐
   Parole Officer ☐
   Parolee ☐
   Volunteer ☐
   Other: ☐

2. What is your understanding regarding the purpose of the Volunteer Services provided: _____

3. How did you hear about this Volunteer Services Program? _____

4. Do you feel the volunteers you have met have, in performing their service, demonstrated:

	YES	NO
Organization	☐	☐
Responsibility	☐	☐
Sincerity	☐	☐
Qualified Backgrounds	☐	☐

Comments: _____

	YES	NO
5. Do you find that this volunteer service interfered with the regularly scheduled programs and services of the Department?	☐	☐
6. Do you feel the rules and regulations of the Department prevented volunteers from providing the best possible services?	☐	☐
7. Were you given any kind of orientation or training?	☐	☐

If Yes, by whom?

Correctional Staff ☐
Volunteer Services Program Staff ☐
Other Volunteers ☐
Other ☐

YES NO

8. Do you feel the training was adequate? ☐ ☐

Comments: _____

_____

9. In general, do you think the Volunteer Services provided was worthwhile? ☐ ☐

10. Should this volunteer service be:

Expanded ☐
Continued in present form ☐
Continued but with changes ☐
Discontinued ☐

Comments: _____

_____

11. What additional volunteer services do you feel could be provided by the Community?

_____

_____

_____

_____

_____
Signature (Optional)

_____
Date

APPENDIX Q: 101 ways to give recognition to volunteers*

Continuously, but always inconclusively, the subject of recognition is discussed by directors and coordinators of volunteer programs. There is great agreement as to its importance but great diversity in its implementation.

Listed below are 101 possibilities gathered from hither and yon. The duplication at 1 and 101 is for emphasis. The blank at 102 is for the beginning of your own list.

I think it is important to remember that recognition is not so much something you do as it is something you are. It is a sensitivity to others as persons, not a strategy for discharging obligations.

1. Smile.
2. Put up a volunteer suggestion box.
3. Treat them to a soda.
4. Reimburse assignment-related expenses.
5. Ask for a report.
6. Send a birthday card.
7. Arrange for discounts.
8. Give service stripes.
9. Maintain a coffee bar.
10. Plan annual ceremonial occasions.
11. Invite them to staff meetings.
12. Recognize personal needs and problems.
13. Accommodate personal needs and problems.
14. Be pleasant.
15. Use them in an emergency situation.
16. Provide a baby sitter.
17. Post Honor Roll in reception area.
18. Respect their wishes.
19. Give informal teas.
20. Keep challenging them.
21. Send a Thanksgiving Day card to the volunteer's family.
22. Provide a nursery.
23. Say "Good Morning."
24. Greet them by name.
25. Provide good preservice training.
26. Help develop self-confidence.

Vern Lake, Volunteer Services Consultant, Minnesota Department of Public Welfare.

27. Award plaques to sponsoring group.

28. Take time to explain fully.

29. Be verbal.

30. Motivate agency VIPs to converse with them.

31. Hold rap sessions.

32. Give additional responsibility.

33. Afford participation in team planning.

34. Respect sensitivities.

35. Enable them to grow on the job.

36. Enable them to grow out of the job.

37. Send newsworthy information to the media.

38. Have wine and cheese tasting parties.

39. Ask client-patient to evaluate their work-service.

40. Say "Good Afternoon."

41. Honor their preferences.

42. Create pleasant surroundings.

43. Welcome them to staff coffee breaks.

44. Enlist them to train other volunteers.

45. Have a public reception.

46. Take time to talk.

47. Defend against hostile or negative staff.

48. Make good plans

49. Commend them to supervisory staff.

50. Send a valentine.

51. Make thorough prearrangements.

52. Persuade "personnel" to equate volunteer experience with work experience.

53. Admit to partnership with paid staff.

54. Recommend them to prospective employer.

55. Provide scholarships to volunteer conferences or workshops.

56. Offer advocacy roles.

57. Utilize them as consultants.

58. Write them thank you notes.

59. Invite their participation in policy formulation.

60. Surprise them with coffee and cake.

61. Celebrate outstanding projects and achievements.

62. Nominate them for volunteer awards.

63. Have a "Presidents Day" for new presidents of sponsoring groups.

64. Carefully match volunteer with job.

65. Praise them to their friends.

66. Provide substantive inservice training.

67. Provide useful tools in good working condition.

68. Say "Good Night."

69. Plan staff and volunteer social events.

70. Be a *real* person.

71. Rent billboard space for public laudation.

72. Accept their individuality.

73. Provide opportunities for conferences and evaluation.

74. Identify age groups.

75. Maintain meaningful file.

76. Send impromptu fun cards.

77. Plan occasional extravaganzas.

78. Instigate client planned surprises.

79. Utilize purchased newspaper space.

80. Promote a "Volunteer-of-the-Month" program.

81. Send letter of appreciation to employer.

82. Plan a "Recognition Edition" of the agency newsletter.

83. Color code name tags to indicate particular achievements (hours, years, unit, etc.)

84. Send commendatory letters to prominent public figures.

85. Say "we missed you."

86. Praise the sponsoring group or club.

87. Promote staff smiles.

88. Facilitate personal maturation.

89. Distinguish between groups and individuals in the group.

90. Maintain safe working conditions.

91. Adequately orientate them.

92. Award special citations for extraordinary achievements.

93. Fully indoctrinate them regarding the agency.

94. Send Christmas cards.

95. Be familiar with the details of their assignments.

96. Conduct community-wide, cooperative, inter-agency recognition events.

97. Plan a theater party.

98. Attend a sports event.

99. Have a picnic.

100. Say "Thank You."

101. Smile

102.

A. Costs:
1. Direct
   a. Coordinator's Salary $_____
   b. Recordkeeping/Secretarial _____
   c. Recognition materials _____
   d. Expenses—mileage, meals, etc. _____
   e. Printed materials _____
   f. Office supplies _____
   g. Insurance _____
   h. Other _____

   Total Direct $_____
2. Indirect
   a. Overhead _____
   b. Other staff _____
   c. Equipment _____
   d. Other _____

   Total Indirect $_____

   TOTAL COSTS $_____ (A)

B. Outputs

***

1. Activity = # of Vol. × # of Hours × Rate/hr. = $_____

   a. _____ _____ × _____ × _____ = _____
   b. _____ _____ × _____ × _____ = _____
   c. _____ _____ × _____ × _____ = _____
   d. _____ _____ × _____ × _____ = _____
   e. _____ _____ × _____ × _____ = _____
   f. _____ _____ × _____ × _____ = _____

   Ttl(B) _____ Ttl(C) _____ Ttl(D)$_____

C. Cost Effectiveness Analysis

   Outputs(D)/Costs(A) = 1: _____ ratio
   For every $ spent, $ X of service are provided

D. Other Calculations

   Cost(A)/# of vol.(B) = cost per vol.

   Cost(A)/# of clients served = cost per client

   Cost(A)/# of hours volunteered(C) = cost per service hour

***Rate could be: Minimum wage $3.35/hr
                    Equivalency (i.e., school teacher $18,000/year
                    =8.65/hr.) Full time equivalent = 2,080 hours
                    Average median salary or average wage of agency
                    = _____
                    Professional average (i.e., $60/hr. lawyer)

APPENDIX S: Dollar worth of volunteers, youth soccer, boys 8 and under*

PRACTICE: 5 week times 2 practice =   10
                10 times 1.5 hrs.   =   15 hrs.
                15 times 2 coaches   =   30 hrs.
                30 hrs. times $4.00   = $120
               120 times 10 teams   = $1200.00

LEAGUE GAMES: 60 games times 1.5 hrs. = 90 hrs.
                  90 hrs. times 4 coaches = 130 hrs.
               360 hours times $4.00   = $1440.00

                $1200 Hours of practice
                <u>1400</u> Hours of league games
                2640
                  <u>264</u> + 10% benefits
                $2904 Total

*Division one, one league, one season

APPENDIX T: What board members need to know

HERE IS A CHECKLIST OF INFORMATION which should put you "on top" of the organizational situation. You will need copies of most of these documents, answers to the questions and notes on the information to which you can readily refer.

_____ Up-to-date bylaws

_____ An up-to-date list of BOARD MEMBERS with addresses and phone numbers of each

_____ Up-to-date COMMITTEE list including all assignments of board and staff members

_____ A list of VOLUNTEER SERVICES with a description of the work they contribute to your organization

_____ If you are a Committee Chair, do you have your committee's last year's working papers? Minutes, budget, program and evaluations?

_____ Plans for the YEAR'S PROGRAM. What are the year's commitments? What is ongoing? What is new?

_____ Job descriptions (written) of all staff

_____ The written personnel policies of the organization

_____ The written policies as determined by the board

_____ Full information with regard to how your local organization relates to your NATIONAL ORGANIZATION. (If you have a State or Regional organization, the following questions also apply).

    _____ Is your local an affiliate or a branch? (There is a difference in autonomy.)

    _____ What responsibilities does your local have to national? In funds? In reporting?

    _____ What services does your national offer to your local:

        _____ consulting on problems   _____ fund-raising help

        _____ organizational manuals   _____ staff training

        _____ standards of operations   _____ volunteer training (direct

        _____ continuous information   service/board)
        service

_____ List of all—repeat, ALL—sources of FUNDING

_____ Are BENEFITS in force for all staff members?

    _____ Social Security   _____ Insurance

    _____ Retirement   _____ Worker's compensation

_____ Is an ANNUAL AUDIT done by a competent CPA who is *not* on the board?

    _____ Is it fully and accurately reported to the board?

    _____ Accepted by a *vote* of the board?

    _____ Available to any member of the organization?

    _____ To any community citizen?

_____ Do you understand the legal responsibilities of the board of the nonprofit corporation? If not, your board may wish to call in the lawyer who serves your organization.

The following are some of the IMPORTANT LEGAL matters every board member needs to understand:

_____ The incorporation papers of your nonprofit corporation. Laws vary from state to state. You should know exactly how your organization is set up.

_____ Are all CONTRACTS made by your organization in order and up to date?

    _____ With staff? Individually? With their union or professional group which bargains for them?

_____With United Way organization? (If your organization is a member)

_____With your national organization, if any?

_____With your landlord, your lease or real estate contract?

_____With the government, military or other organizations funding or purchasing your services?

_____ Are the stipulations of each grant being fully complied with in areas of administration, disbursement, program and reporting?

_____ Is your INSURANCE adequate and in force?

_____ On your building, office, or other facilities?

_____ For your office equipment, etc.?

_____ For your staff?

_____ For your volunteers?

_____ Is this carried nationally or locally?

The domain of the Board and the domain of the administrative staff should be clearly spelled out:

_____Who hires personnel and at what level?

_____Other?

ADAPTED FROM: *The Board Member: Decision Maker for the Nonprofit Organization* by Pauline L. Hanson and Carolyn T. Marmaduke, Han/Mar Publications, 1972.